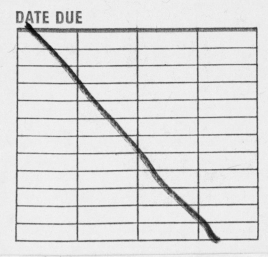

A study sponsored by

Educational Testing Service

*Center for Research and Development in Higher Education
University of California, Berkeley*

College Entrance Examination Board

Beyond the Open Door

*New Students
to Higher Education*

K. Patricia Cross

BEYOND THE OPEN DOOR

Jossey-Bass Inc., Publishers

San Francisco · Washington · London · 1974

BEYOND THE OPEN DOOR
New Students to Higher Education
by K. Patricia Cross

Copyright © 1974 by: Jossey-Bass, Inc., Publishers
615 Montgomery Street
San Francisco, California 94111
&
Jossey-Bass Limited
3 Henrietta Street
London WC2E 8LU

Library of Congress Catalogue Card Number LC 77-170212

International Standard Book Number ISBN 0-87589-111-X

Manufactured in the United States of America

JACKET DESIGN BY WILLI BAUM

FIRST EDITION
First Printing: November 1971
Second Printing: November 1972
Third Printing: November 1974

Code 7133

The
Jossey-Bass Series
in Higher Education

Consulting Editor

HAROLD L. HODGKINSON
University of California, Berkeley

PREFACE

America has made a commitment to open the door to educational opportunity to all of her citizens. The opening of that door—even three quarters of the way—is a significant accomplishment, but it is not enough. For some students who have been underrepresented in colleges, the door to traditional postsecondary education opens only on more of the same kind of education that has failed to serve them in the past. *Beyond the Open Door* seeks to shed some light on the critical task of developing an education that will serve the needs of New Students to higher education.

Chapter One analyzes the changing philosophies over the years as the nation has attempted to address itself to the question: Who should go to college? It then speaks to the question: Who is going to college now? Finally, it makes some predictions about who will go to college.

Chapter Two shows how educational experiences in the American school system have differed for New Students and traditional students. It suggests that the failure experiences of New Students have resulted in a different approach to learning from that used by the more successful traditional students.

Chapters Three through Six provide a research description of New Students. In these chapters I seek to answer questions such as these: What are the interests of New Students? How do their aspirations, their attitudes, their values, and their personality characteristics differ from those of more traditional students? What do they think about their past education and what do they expect of postsecondary education? What are their career aspirations, and how do they expect education to prepare them for their futures?

Chapter Seven utilizes data from a national sample of youth who were retested one year and five years after their graduations from high school. Some of these young people were the predecessors of the present generation of New Students. What paths did these young people follow? How satisfying is life to them? What would they have done differently? How well did education serve them?

Chapters Eight and Nine are concerned with two groups of young people (ethnic minorities and women) who are new to higher education but who do not necessarily fall in the category used for the research descriptions in Chapters Three through Seven—those ranking in the lowest third of the high school graduating classes on tests of academic ability.

Finally, Chapter Ten makes some specific suggestions and recommendations about how the presence of New Students should change postsecondary education.

The central thesis of this book is that there is a New Student to higher education and that institutions of higher education are not prepared to educate him. Traditional education has failed him in the past; and, unless substantial changes are made, it will fail him in the future. Initially, I undertook this project in the hope that an understanding of New Students would help in creating improved educational programs at the *postsecondary* level. As the work progressed, however, it became clear that many of the learning problems of these students were directly attributable to school experiences at the elementary and secondary levels. Therefore, the implications of the research findings have relevance for the restructuring of education at all levels.

A few details about the design of this project: From the beginning, I have operated under the assumption that researchers have already collected more information about students than has been used. I therefore vowed not to collect new data from students. Rather, I built the study from a foundation consisting of data collected in four major research projects conducted between 1960 and 1969. All four of the data banks represent large, nationally diverse, but not necessarily nationally representative, samples of students. Three utilize longitudinal designs following high school students into postsecondary education; one is a data bank of information collected from students entering two-year colleges. The studies were not designed to be comparable; the measuring instruments are not the same; the dependent variables differ from study to study. Yet the groups designated New Students are remarkably similar across the four samples. Although the use of four major studies results in a surfeit of information, the consistency of patterns gives assurance that the findings are not artifacts of the particular data bank used. A summary description of each of the projects is presented in Appendix A. Briefly, the four data banks that form the central information system from which the research description of New Students is culled are as follows: (1) Project TALENT, a national sample of 62,602 high school seniors tested in the spring of 1960 with follow-up studies in 1961 and 1965. (2) The Growth Study, a diverse sample of 8,891 students tested as high school juniors in 1965 preceded by data collections in 1961 and 1963, when the students were seventh and ninth graders, and followed up in 1967 and 1968, when the students were high school seniors and one year beyond high school graduation. (3) SCOPE (School to College: Opportunity for Postsecondary Education), a four-state sample of 33,879 high school seniors tested in 1966 with a 1967 follow-up collection of data. (4) Comparative Guidance and Placement Program (CGP), a sample of 23,719 entrants tested by forty-five community colleges in 1969.

The analyses presented in Chapter One led me to the conclusion that the distinguishing characteristic of the young people seeking postsecondary education in the 1970s is their low level of academic achievement on traditional measures in traditional curricula. Therefore, for each of the four data sources, New Students were defined as those scoring in the lowest third of the sample on a conventional test of academic achievement, whereas traditional students were those scoring in the upper third. New Students are referred to during the presentation of research data as lowest-third or low-A students, where the "A" stands for academic aptitude, ability, or achievement. Appendix B describes key characteristics of these young people in each of the four basic data sources.

My purpose in writing *Beyond the Open Door* is to help educational practitioners improve educational programs provided for New Students. Although it is a report of research, it is not written primarily for scientists but rather for graduate students; teachers in high schools, community colleges, and four-year institutions; administrators; legislators; and anyone else interested in improving the practice of education. My goal has been to present and interpret research data in a manner that is interesting to read, easy to understand, and practical to apply. While I may have fallen short of that ideal, it may help the reader if I make explicit some of the choices that I made in reaching toward my goal of communicating with an intended audience that I perceive as educationally sophisticated but not necessarily trained in research methods and terminology.

First, precision of the language of research has sometimes been slighted in favor of readability. For example, the reader may see phrases such as "bright but poor students" in place of the more precise "students scoring in the top quarter of the sample on a traditional test of academic ability but in the lowest quarter on an index of socioeconomic status." Mindful, however, that *Beyond the Open Door* is also addressed to people who need to know precisely how the groups were defined, I have not used the briefer phrases where I felt that there could be any doubt about the actual meaning.

Second, powerful and complex statistical methods were sacrificed in favor of those that could be understood easily by educators without research training. No statistical treatment used is more complicated than a simple percentage. The reader may assume that anything treated as educationally significant has been checked to be sure that it is statistically significant. In the huge samples used in these analyses, however, even a difference of 1 or 2 per cent is likely to be statistically significant, and the criterion of educational significance is more rigorous than that of statistical significance.

Third, although I am confident that any interpretation of the data is responsible, to the best of my ability to judge, I have leaned toward making interpretations freely rather than cautiously. It is my conviction that we may make better progress by acting upon the basis of what the data suggest rather than waiting for proof. Precious little of what we do now has ever been "proved," and perhaps nothing will be lost by acting upon some suggested assumptions.

My indebtedness to many people is very great. This book would not have been written were it not for the cooperation of three generous sponsors: Educational Testing Service; the Center for

Research and Development in Higher Education of the University of California, Berkeley; and the College Entrance Examination Board. Leland L. Medsker, director of the Center for Research and Development in Higher Education, and Robert J. Solomon, executive vice president of Educational Testing Service, are two valued friends and colleagues whose interest and support have been unwavering throughout the year and a half that was required for collecting and organizing the data and committing my learning to writing.

Long years of professional lifetimes and enormous amounts of work had gone into the design and collection of research data before I even started my work. I cannot begin to thank all the people—most of them unknown to me—who contributed in diverse ways to the team research that made possible the gold mines of information contained in Project TALENT, SCOPE, the Growth Study, and the Comparative Guidance and Placement program.

Dale Tillery, of the Center for Research and Development in Higher Education, has been the chief architect and the director of the SCOPE project throughout the six years of its life under the sponsorship of the College Entrance Examination Board. He and Denis Donovon have been very generous with their data, their time, and their talent. Charles Gehrke, director of data processing for the Center, provided the expertise that turned raw data into information about New Students. Thomas Hilton, senior research psychologist of Educational Testing Service, is the director of the longitudinal Growth Study. He and his staff have been most cooperative in making these data freely available to me. The empirical analyses of the effects of failure presented in Chapter Two would not have been possible without the careful collection of data on cognitive development over a five-year period by the staff of the Growth Study.

John Claudy, director of the Project TALENT data bank, handled the complex subgroup analyses of the TALENT data. Probably the most ambitious longitudinal study of young people ever undertaken, Project TALENT served as the pioneering model for longitudinal studies of the education of young people, and it remains a vast source of knowledge about the developmental processes of growing up.

The youngest data bank to contribute to the research description of New Studies is the Comparative Guidance and Placement Program (CGP). Sponsored by the College Entrance Examination Board and administered by Educational Testing Service, CGP is the New Students' data bank. More than any other source, CGP is directed toward measuring the special abilities and interests of New Students to higher education. My appreciation is extended to the present director of CGP, Elizabeth Stewart, and to her predecessor, Alice Irby, both of Educational Testing Service, for their attention to my requests during the hectic days when they were coping with the excitement and frustration of launching the new program.

My research colleagues at both Educational Testing Service and the Center of Research and Development in Higher Education have been consistently generous with their time and helpful in reading and criticizing drafts and discussing issues. My special gratitude is extended to Edwin Klingelhofer, visiting research psychologist at the Center. A gentle and perceptive critic, he generously read most of the manuscript, and his comments proved exceptionally valuable to me.

Sincere appreciation is also extended to Abraham Carp, Harold Hodgkinson, Richard Peterson, Rodney Reed, George Temp, and Jonathan Warren, all of whom read drafts of one or more chapters and whose insights and knowledge improved the final version.

Dorothy Roy, of Educational Testing Service, with enormous patience and efficiency turned countless penciled tablets into neat typescript; and Mildred Bowman and Linda Brubaker, manuscript typists at the Center, prepared the final manuscript. Shelly Buck, research assistant in 1970, helped to launch the project, and her perceptive search of the literature provided the background for the interpretation of the new data. Margaret Elliott, of Educational Testing Service, worked with resourcefulness and unfailing good humor on the myriad details involved in preparing final copy for publication.

Berkeley   K. PATRICIA CROSS
October 1971

CONTENTS

BEYOND THE OPEN DOOR

New Students to Higher Education

NEW STUDENTS
OF THE 1970s

1

Who should go to college? Who is going to college? Who will go to college?

Planning for New Students to higher education in the 1970s requires an answer to the last question posed above. Only when we fully understand the answer to that question can we design appropriate educational experiences for college students of the near future. But the complex answer to that question begins with a synthesis of the answers to the first two questions. The question Who should go to college? is one to be answered by society; the question Who is going to college? can be answered by research. When we can describe who is going to college and when we can reach some consensus on who should go to college, then we can determine who will go to college and we can begin to plan accordingly.

Who Should Go to College

In the history of higher education in this country there have been three major philosophies about who should go to college. When the country was young, most college students came from the homes of wealthy "aristocrats." Students who attended colleges—private high-

1

tuition colleges: Harvard, Yale, Princeton—had money and family social status. Some also had academic interests and abilities; others did not. Basic to the aristocratic philosophy of college admissions was the premise that the young people who should go to college were those who could afford it and who needed it for their station in life. The poor, ethnic minorities, and women, it was assumed, would not follow life patterns that made use of a college education (although a number of finishing colleges for women had as their purpose the training of young ladies to take their place in the aristocracy).

The revolt against aristocratic philosophies of college admissions was led by those who maintained that a college education is an earned right, not a birthright. Champions of the new land-grant universities, which heralded the rise of the meritocracy, questioned the traditional role of tuition; and they had some unconventional ideas about the curricula that would serve the needs of a new clientele. The working man, they claimed, should be able to send his children to college. And the young people should be able to prepare themselves for professional careers through the pursuit of a course of studies much broader than that offered by the aristocratic colleges of the time.

Advocates of the meritocracy felt that criteria for college admission should be based upon scholastic ability and the willingness to study hard—in short, upon academic merit. In practice, meritocratic principles were applied by means of rather narrow criteria of grades and test scores to define merit and to select the "most promising" young people to attend college. Philosophically, the meritocracy reached its peak in the 1950s. The pervading philosophy of that time is typified by an assertion made in a well-known study by the Commission on Human Resources and Advanced Training:

The democratic ideal is one of equal opportunity; within that ideal it is both individually advantageous and socially desirable for each person to make the best possible use of his talents. But equal opportunity does not mean equal accomplishments or identical use. Some men have greater ability than others and can accomplish things which are beyond the powers of men of lesser endowment. . . . The nation needs to make effective use of its intellec-

tual resources. To do so means to use well its brightest people whether they come from farm or city, from the slum section or the country club area, regardless of color or religious or economic differences but not regardless of ability [*Wolfle, 1954, p. 6, emphasis added*].

Much as the aristocratic colleges had assumed that their curriculum was static and designed for an elite portion of the population, so the colleges of the meritocracy assumed that only a fairly small portion of the population had the ability to benefit from what they offered. Considerable attention was given in the late 1940s and early 1950s to determining the actual size of this group. The President's Advisory Commission on Higher Education of 1947 estimated that 49 per cent of the population could profit from at least two years of post–high school education and that about 32 per cent had the capacity for a normal four-year-college course. After considering this figure, in conjunction with the observation that "most experts estimate that about 25 per cent of the population can do college work profitably," Hollinshead's report for the Commission on Financing Higher Education (1952) concluded: "Perhaps 35 per cent of youth might be expected to profit substantially from formal full-time post–high school education of the kind given at present by such institutions" (p. 138). According to these Commissions, then, the proportion of the population that could benefit from further education was much larger than had previously been assumed. It took less than two decades to surpass what appeared to them very liberal estimates of the numbers of persons who should be and would be attending college.

The rise of the meritocracy was generally regarded as a move that, in the best traditions of the country, led to the democratization of higher education, the breaking down of barriers imposed by the aristocracy. Ironically, however, advocates of the meritocracy were systematically erecting their own barriers. Academic-aptitude tests served both to destroy the old barriers and to erect new barriers to college admission. The talent searches of the 1950s were active campaigns to bring into the colleges those who did not meet aristocratic criteria but who epitomized meritocratic ideals. The very good student who was the son of an immigrant cobbler was the hero of the meritocracy—no money, no family social status, but lots of academic talent and a willingness to work hard.

In the early 1970s the prevailing attitude in the country appears still largely meritocratic, but there are signs everywhere of a straining at the barriers. Once again there is pressure to democratize higher education by bringing it within reach of a broader segment of the population. Once again there are demands for new answers to the old question of what proportion of the population the colleges should serve. A new sector of the public is being represented by New Students in colleges and universities. These New Students to higher education are repeating history by entering the system—not so much by breaking down the barriers erected by the meritocracy (although there is some of that) as by flocking to a new kind of college dedicated to serving a different clientele.

The mingling of meritocratic and egalitarian philosophies is the cause of considerable controversy among educators as well as in the popular press. The sign of the times is illustrated by a headline (*Time,* 1970) reading: "Open Admissions: American Dream or Disaster?" At the same time that the formerly selective, tuition-free City University of New York was instituting egalitarianism by throwing open its doors to all 1970 New York City high school graduates, regardless of academic qualifications, the 1970 President's Task Force on Higher Education was embracing meritocracy and attempting to clear away the last vestiges of the aristocratic era by recommending financial aid to "students of all races who have the desire and *ability to profit* from post–high school education" (italics added). John Gardner has asked, Can we be equal and excellent too? Can egalitarianism and meritocracy coexist? What happens to the value of the college degree when everyone has one? Is there some fixed concept of "college" that permits us to say who should attend? Should higher education serve those who can profit from traditional offerings, or is there an obligation to change the offerings to meet the needs of those who wish to attend college?

To date, we have concentrated on making New Students over into the image of traditional students, so that they can be served by traditional education. Our concern has been the creation

of access models to education.[1] We have devised all kinds of ways to
make New Students eligible to participate in *traditional* higher education. Remedial courses are designed to remove academic "deficiencies"; counseling removes motivational "deficiencies"; financial
aid removes financial "deficiencies." However, if the answer to the
question Who should go to college? is to be an egalitarian response
of "everyone," then educational systems will have to be designed to
fit the learning needs of New Students.

In short, the gap between New Students and traditional
higher education is large; it can be narrowed by moving students
and education toward each other. That is the subject of this book.

Who Is Going to College?

Who are the young people entering college today? Or, perhaps more important, who are the young people *not* entering
college? We do not know the full dimensions of the answer to this
question, but the question could be answered rather accurately,
given enough money, enough research talent, enough cooperation,
and enough patience and persistence. These ingredients, however,
are not easily come by; and the number of longitudinal research
studies (studies that follow young people as they graduate from high
school and enter or do not enter college) is not large. Furthermore,
the studies that have been done vary somewhat with the nature of
the sample and the date of the study. Nevertheless, the major results
are sufficiently consistent to give us considerable confidence in what
we know about the effects of socioeconomic status and academic
aptitude upon educational attainment.

Most laymen recognize that bright high school graduates are
more likely to continue their education than those who have had to
struggle for grades throughout high school, that doctors' sons are
more likely than laborers' sons to attend college, that whites are
more likely than blacks, and that men are more likely than women
to seek further education. These elements of the folk wisdom about
who goes to college are by no means independent. Young people
are more likely to suffer multiple disadvantages or to enjoy multiple
privileges than they are to exhibit a balance of advantages and dis-

---

[1] For a discussion of some alternatives, see Cross (1971).

advantages. For example, it is highly probable that a young person belonging to an ethnic minority also ranks low in socioeconomic status (SES) and in academic ability. It is also highly probable that the son of a wealthy executive belongs to the ethnic majority and scores high on a test of academic aptitude.

Of the dimensions that researchers have been able to measure, SES (which includes measures of family occupation and parental education) and academic ability hold primary places in explaining who goes to college, where, and for how long. And, as data from the Project TALENT sample of high school seniors indicate, SES and academic aptitude are closely related. When Project TALENT high school seniors were classified by academic ability and SES, 83 per cent of the low-SES group scored low on the test and 79 per cent of the high-SES students scored high. These data, of course, show *only* that SES and ability-test scores are closely related; they do not show that the low test scores of low-SES youth are *caused* by low intelligence or by their low SES or that tests are biased against those of low SES.

Some of the most important data on the relationships between SES, ability, and college attendance were presented by Sewell and Shah (1967) for a sample of 1957 Wisconsin high school graduates and by Schoenfeldt (1968) for Project TALENT high school graduates of 1961. Recently, Hilton, using the same scheme of tabulation, analyzed ETS Growth Study data for 1967 high school graduates. Although the samples are different, the patterns reveal three major barriers to higher education—low socioeconomic level, low tested academic aptitude, and female sex. A fourth major barrier, minority ethnic status, is not amenable to study in these data, but it is examined in Chapter 8.

Table 1 shows the three sets of data side by side. While the differences in the samples of the three projects warn against over-dependence on specific figures, the similarity of patterns provides reassurance that the data are not artifacts of the sample tested. These sets of data were not designed to be comparable,[2] but we can be rather certain of some things. For example, the probability is ex-

[2] See Appendix A for descriptions of Project TALENT and ETS Growth Study samples; see Sewell and Shah (1967) for a description of the Wisconsin High School Graduate Study.

Table 1. High School Graduates Attending Two- or Four-Year Colleges

	Socioeconomic Quarter											
	1 (low)			2			3			4 (high)		
Ability Quarter	1957[a]	1961[b]	1967[c]	1957	1961	1967	1957	1961	1967	1957	1961	1967
	Per Cent			Per Cent			Per Cent			Per Cent		
Male												
1 (low)	6	9	33	12	14	30	18	16	29	39	34	57
2	17	16	43	27	25	39	34	36	55	61	45	61
3	28	32	60	43	38	69	51	48	68	73	72	79
4 (high)	52	58	75	59	74	80	72	79	89	91	90	92
Female												
1 (low)	4	8	25	9	12	28	16	13	36	33	26	37
2	6	13	28	20	12	36	26	21	50	44	37	67
3	9	25	44	24	30	48	31	40	68	67	65	77
4 (high)	28	34	60	37	51	73	48	71	83	76	85	93

[a] 1957 graduates, with 1964 follow-up; Sewell and Shah (1967).
[b] 1961 graduates, with 1962 follow-up; Schoenfeldt (1968).
[c] 1967 graduates, with 1968 follow-up; ETS Growth Study data analysis by Thomas Hilton.

tremely high that the son of a surgeon who has been an *A* student in high school will go to college. For males ranking in the top quarter on *both* SES and ability, there is little fluctuation in the three sets of data: 90–92 per cent have entered college. For top-quarter girls in both SES and ability, it is the pattern of *growth* that is remarkable. In the 1957 Wisconsin data, only three fourths of this group were entering two- or four-year colleges; the 1961 Project TALENT sample showed 85 per cent; and the 1967 ETS data reported 93 per cent. Although the differences in sampling procedures prevent any precise statement on the rate of growth for high-SES–high-ability women, we can be quite confident that the percentage of women in this group attending college in 1968 had reached near saturation, and that this was not the case for women ten years earlier. In the 1970s very few additional college students are to be expected from among high school graduates who are high in both academic aptitude and socioeconomic status.

At the other extreme are the doubly disadvantaged—those scoring in the lowest quarter on both SES and ability. For example, in the 1961 TALENT sample, only 9 per cent of the lowest-quarter males in both SES and ability entered college in the fall following high school graduation. If we knew nothing about a boy except that he made lowest-quarter test scores and came from a home where the father had little education and worked at a menial job, we could predict with a high degree of accuracy that at the beginning of the 1960s he would *not* go to college. We would have been correct nine times out of ten.

Forecasts made for individuals in the middle cells are considerably less accurate. For example, we know that 60 per cent of the boys in the lowest SES quarter of the 1967 Growth Study sample who scored in the third ability quarter on the test entered college in 1968. If, armed with test score and SES index, we guessed that any individual student in that group would enter college, we would be right six times out of ten—or barely better than chance.

We can say with considerable confidence, however, that low-SES boys are much more likely to enter college if they have done well in school in the past (or, more accurately, scored high on a test related to school performance). In the 1967 sample, for example, 75 per cent of the boys in the *lowest* SES quarter entered college if they scored in the highest quarter in ability. That figure, incidentally, is testimony to the existence of the meritocracy. Male students of high "merit" are likely to get to college today regardless of socioeconomic background. But the operation of the aristocracy is also evident; if the boy with high merit had high socioeconomic status, his chances would have been nearer 92 per cent.

Table 2 illustrates the extent of participation in the broad spectrum of postsecondary education. Data from the 1958 study were not available in this form, but 1961 and 1967 data show the percentages of young people continuing their formal education in trade schools, business colleges, and armed forces schools as well as in two-year and four-year colleges.

The figures for males in this table show quite clearly the full flowering of the meritocratic era in postsecondary education. The data for women, however, show stronger evidence of aristocratic practices. High ability is not as likely to compensate for low SES for girls as it is for boys. Sewell and Shah (1967), in their study of Wisconsin youth, also observed the special importance of socioeconomic background for women:

Both socioeconomic status and intelligence have direct effects on planning on college, college attendance, and college graduation, and considerable indirect effect on the level of educational attainment through their effects on college plans and college attendance. However, for females the relative effect of socioeconomic status on college plans, college attendance, and college graduation was greater than was the effect of intelligence, while for males the relative effect of intelligence at each of these stages was greater than the effect of socioeconomic status [p. 1].

Analyses such as those presented in Tables 1 and 2 permit some further data-based speculation about the trends in higher education during the 1960s. The Growth Study data peg the proportion of high school graduates continuing in some form of postsecondary education at about 70 per cent, with 61 per cent entering two- or four-year colleges. The Growth Study sample was selected to represent the *range* of school systems; but more than half of the subjects resided in large cities, where educational opportunities are more easily accessible than in less populated areas. Thus, although Growth

Table 2. HIGH SCHOOL GRADUATES ENTERING SOME FORM OF POSTSECONDARY EDUCATION

	Socioeconomic Quarter							
	1 (low)		2		3		4 (high)	
Ability Quarter	*Per Cent*		*Per Cent*		*Per Cent*		*Per Cent*	
	1961[a]	1967[b]	1961	1967	1961	1967	1961	1967
Male								
1 (low)	21	48	28	55	30	40	51	65
2	37	57	47	58	51	69	61	79
3	47	74	52	77	66	79	82	88
4 (high)	69	82	83	89	87	93	93	94
Female								
1 (low)	14	39	25	41	26	55	39	60
2	26	40	27	44	41	64	57	76
3	38	52	51	58	54	77	76	86
4 (high)	58	69	66	77	84	88	91	95

[a] 1961 graduates, with 1962 follow-up; Schoenfeldt, 1968.
[b] 1967 graduates, with 1968 follow-up; ETS Growth Study data analysis by Thomas Hilton.

Study data may possibly overrepresent national college-going rates, some of the most recent studies (published and unpublished) suggest that these data reflect rather accurately the extremely rapid approach of universal postsecondary education—especially in the most populous states, which tend to lead the country into new eras. A well-designed study of New York State high school seniors showed 67 per cent planning in June 1968 to continue postsecondary education the following fall, with 59 per cent planning to enter two- or four-year colleges (University of the State of New York, 1969). In California, with its extensive development of public higher education, 80 per cent of the high school graduates are reported entering college (Hitch, 1970). But when this ratio is examined by geographical region, there is great variation—attributable in part to the higher education facilities available in the region. Willingham (1970) reported the ratio of degree-credit college freshmen to high school graduates in 1968 as ranging from 0.52 in the South to 0.69 in the West.

The egalitarian era is rapidly approaching; most young people are already pursuing postsecondary education. Although the major concern of educators at the present time is with *access* to higher education, these data, as well as those presented in later chapters, indicate that, for men at least, low academic ability is keeping more students from continuing their education than is the barrier of lack of financial resources. Continued emphasis on access programs will bring increasing numbers of low-ability students into programs of postsecondary education. Traditional college programs are not prepared to handle the learning needs of these New Students to higher education.

Who Will Go to College?

The pressures are strong for an egalitarian philosophy of access to postsecondary education. Egalitarians maintain that anyone who wants to pursue further education should be helped to do so, regardless of economic resources and regardless of past academic achievement. Adoption of egalitarian practices would in effect abolish the effectiveness of present major predictors of college entrance—SES and academic aptitude. If the meritocracy is ebbing and egalitarianism is on the rise, who *will* go to college?

Although the description is not quite accurate, it is generally conceded that we have in this country a system of universal secondary education, wherein young people who are physically and mentally able to attend high school do so. In reality, only about 80 per cent of the young people graduate from high school. If we assume that universal higher education will exist when it becomes as common as high school graduation is today—that is, when 80 per cent of the high school graduates continue their education—then we may construct a hypothetical egalitarian form of Table 2 wherein every SES-ability cell has an 80 per cent probability for postsecondary education. Thus, 80 per cent of those in the top quarter on both SES and ability would continue their education, and 80 per cent of those in the bottom quarter on both indices would also continue in some form of postsecondary education. Table 2 shows that, in such a model, we already have universal postsecondary education for males in the top ability quarter, since 80 per cent of the highly able male high school graduates continue their education beyond high school. Table 3 shows the reservoir of potential New Students to higher education. It is obtained by subtracting the 1967 percentages in each cell of Table 2 (the reality) from 80 (ideal egalitarianism).

Quite clearly, most of the New Students would come from rows 1 and 2—the lower half of the class academically. There would be almost no additional males from the upper half of the class, although there would be a significant number of women who stand in the top half of the class academically—almost all of them from the lower half of the socioeconomic scale.

New Students to higher education will be primarily students whose performance at academic tasks in the past has been below average. Low academic ability, as that ability is traditionally nurtured and measured in the schools, will be the distinguishing characteristic of these students. We have not yet faced the full meaning of this prediction. Many educators as well as the general public are still thinking of New Students largely in ethnic terms. True, black college enrollments have more than doubled since the mid-1960s, and they will need to double again before equality of educational opportunity approaches reality. Other ethnic groups have even further to go. As many college teachers know, however, educational

Table 3. HYPOTHETICAL RESERVOIR* OF POTENTIAL STUDENTS
FOR ATTAINMENT OF EGALITARIAN POSTSECONDARY EDUCATION

	Socioeconomic Quarter			
Ability Quarter	1 (low)	2	3	4 (high)
Male				
1 (low)	32	25	40	15
2	23	22	11	1
3	6	3	1	—
4 (high)	—	—	—	—
Female				
1 (low)	41	33	25	20
2	40	36	16	4
3	18	12	3	—
4 (high)	11	3	—	—

* 80 per cent minus the percentage in each cell of the 1967
ETS Growth Study data presented in Table 2.

problems are not color-bound. Two thirds of the community colleges
surveyed in the spring of 1971 stated that less than one fourth of the
students enrolled in "remedial" classes were members of ethnic
minorities (Appendix C).

New Students Defined

New Students to higher education, as they are discussed in
this book, are operationally defined as those scoring in the lowest
third among national samples of young people on traditional tests of
academic ability. Women and young people from ethnic minorities
are also New Students, but their special problems as members of
minority groups in higher education are discussed in Chapters 8 and
9. When they also score low on conventional tests, they are included
in the primary concern of this book—New Students for whom
present forms of education are inappropriate.

The definition of New Students as those scoring low on traditional tests of academic ability may at first seem unacceptable to some readers. Therefore, let me make explicit the reasons for this decision. The primary reason is the very obvious one already discussed. Young people who have not considered college in the past but who are newly entering college in the 1970s are distinguished more by low test scores than by any other single measure available, including race, sex, and socioeconomic status.

Second, New Students have *educational* problems; they do not perform traditional educational tasks with competence. Despite widely circulated myths of test bias, it stands to reason that the individual who has difficulty performing the tasks called for on traditional tests of academic ability is likely to have difficulty performing similar tasks in the classroom. Furthermore, there is now good research evidence that tests are moderately good predictors of college grades—as good for members of minority groups as for majority youth (see Chapter 8).

High school grades might have been used, instead of tests, to define the group of students whom traditional education has failed; but, in the national samples used herein, the fluctuation of grades from high school to high school introduces a different kind of problem, and, all things considered, tests seemed to be the best indicators of groups of New Students that will present educational challenges to postsecondary education.

The question to be answered by the research presented in this study is What are the past experiences, aspirations, interests, attitudes, and abilities of New Students to higher education? And, most important, What are their educational needs and interests? Appendix B presents a few selected characteristics of New Students as they appear in each of the four major research studies synthesized in this volume. The groups defined as New Students by four different criterion tests in four diverse samples of students are much more remarkable for their similarities than for their differences. There is indeed a New Student to higher education, and a research profile can be presented. Because people seem to have vivid stereotypes of New Students, it may be useful to present a capsule profile of the backgrounds of typical New Students before embarking upon the more detailed descriptions of their interests, attitudes, and educational and vocational aspirations as these are revealed in self-reports.

Profile of New Students

Most of the New Students described in this book are Caucasians whose fathers work at blue-collar jobs. A substantial number, however, are members of minority ethnic groups. Most of the parents have never attended college, and the expectation of college is new to the family. The New Students themselves have not been especially successful at their high school studies. Whereas traditional college students (upper third) have made *A*'s and *B*'s in high school, New Students have made mostly *C*'s. Traditional students are attracted primarily to four-year colleges and universities, whereas New Students plan to enter public community colleges or vocational schools.

Fundamentally, these New Students to higher education are swept into college by the rising educational aspirations of the citizenry. For the majority, the motivation for college does not arise from anticipation of interest in learning the things they will be learning in college but from the recognition that education is the way to a better job and a better life than that of their parents.

The setting for the description of the characteristics of New Students that follows is best provided by excerpts from a recent study of blue-collar communities—among them, the community of Kensington, which is 99.7 per cent white (Binzen, 1970a). This study presents a succinct picture of the backgrounds of many New Students.

Kensington is a community in crisis. . . . In many ways it looks, thinks, and acts like so many of the Negro ghettos festering in American cities. Its educational, political, social, and economic problems are almost as great as those found in the black slums. It, too, has failed to solve these problems, and failure has made it sullen, surly, and suspicious [p. 2]. . . .

People forget that, in the metropolitan areas, twice as many white as nonwhite families live in "official" poverty, and of course many Whitetowners don't quite qualify for that governmental distinction. They are poor but not poor enough to get help. Usually *earning from $5,000 to $10,000 a year, the Whitetown husband and father works hard as a truck-driver or turret lathe operator or policeman or longshoreman or white-collar clerk—perhaps at more than one of these jobs—to buy and hold on to his fourteen-foot-wide house and new color television set [p. 1]. . . .*

As far as can be told from the scant information available, the children of Whitetown do almost as badly on measurements of academic aptitude and achievement as do the children of the black slums, sometimes slightly worse. In Philadelphia, some inner-city districts that are 90 per cent or more black (North Philadelphia, for example) produce slightly higher test scores than does Kensington's district. Yet Kensington is excluded from such federal programs as Model Cities, and many of its schools fail to qualify for aid under the poverty provision of the Elementary and Secondary Education Act (ESEA) [p. 2].

Although most New Students come from educationally and financially impoverished home backgrounds, many do not. More than a quarter of the young people who have not done well in traditional education are the children of fathers who have attended college. Individually and collectively their learning problems are just as tragic—their sense of school failure is just as pervasive—as those of their financially disadvantaged peers. The very existence of this pool of relatively advantaged students as a significant minority in the New Student group points up the fallacy of assuming that traditional education has served the privileged classes well and the disadvantaged poorly. It would be more accurate to acknowledge that education has served young people with abilities and interests that are developed through traditional academic discipline-bound curricula. The concept of *academic* talent as *the* talent worthy of cultivation and encouragement represents a perspective that is too narrow to provide a base for the development of a new education for the egalitarian age. This book addresses itself to the task of providing a description of New Students that will help us to determine what educational experiences should lie beyond the Open Door.

References

American Council on Education: *A Fact Book on Higher Education: Enrollment Data.* Washington, D.C.: ACE, first issue, 1970.

BINZEN, P. "The World of Whitetown: Neglected Blue-Collar Communities." *Carnegie Quarterly,* Fall 1970, *18* (4), 1–3. a

—————. *Whitetown, U.S.A.* New York: Random House, 1970. b

CROSS, K. P. "Equality of Educational Opportunity." Position paper prepared for the Education Task Force of the White House Conference on Youth, April 18–22, 1971.

FLANAGAN, J. C., AND ASSOCIATES. *Project TALENT: The American High School Student.* Pittsburgh: Project TALENT, University of Pittsburgh, 1964.

HILTON, T. L. Growth Study Data. Princeton: Educational Testing Service. Unpublished.

HITCH, C. J. *California's Master Plan: Some Kind of Education for Nearly Everybody.* Washington, D.C.: American Council on Education, 1970. Mimeographed.

HOLLINSHEAD, B. *Who Should Go to College.* New York: Columbia University Press, 1952.

SCHOENFELDT, L. F. "Education after High School." *Sociology of Education,* 1968, *41* (4), 350–369.

SEWELL, W. H., AND V. P. SHAH. "Socioeconomic Status, Intelligence, and the Attainment of Higher Education." *Sociology of Education,* 1967, *40* (1), 1–23.

Time. "Open Admissions: American Dream or Disaster?" October 19, 1970.

University of the State of New York. *A Longitudinal Study of the Barriers Affecting the Pursuit of Higher Education by New York State High School Seniors.* Phase I. Albany: State Education Department, 1969.

WILLINGHAM, W. *Free-Access Higher Education.* Princeton: College Entrance Examination Board, 1970.

WOLFLE, D. *America's Resources of Specialized Talent.* Report of the Commission on Human Resources and Advanced Training. New York; Harper & Row, 1954.

THE THREAT
OF FAILURE

2

Moving through the American school system is a very different experience for students in the bottom third (low A's) of the class academically than it is for students in the top third (high A's). Since New Students to higher education are coming from the bottom third of the high school graduating classes, it is important to gain some understanding of their past experience with education.

The lowest third *are* learning throughout the years of their elementary and secondary education, but they are learning different lessons from those intended by educators. Most are becoming students of methods to avoid failure. Some of these methods are ingenious; all of them, however, distract attention from learning and are therefore handicapping to future education. An analysis of national dropout statistics may help those who learned English and arithmetic without excessive anxiety to realize how all-pervasive the threat of failure is for those in the lowest third of the class. Relative to other children in school, the below-average youngster in the fifth grade has a much better chance than the above-average child of shifting his position downward by the twelfth grade. The very nature of the dropout statistics constantly threatens the relative position of the lower half of the class while leaving the upper half almost unaffected.

The downward shift of the less apt students is illustrated by figures from the 1960 census. These figures show that for each 1,000 children in the fifth grade, 983 made it to the seventh grade; 966 to the ninth; and, finally, only 721 of the orginal 1,000 graduated from high school. A student ranking 650th out of a hypothetical class of 1,000 fifth graders falls in the middle third of the class. If he still ranks 650th from the top by the time he reaches the twelfth grade, however, he is clearly in the academic cellar, standing 650th out of 721 students. The sorry fact is that if you are next to last, you become last when the last leaves his place, while whoever is first remains unaffected. There is always room at the bottom, it seems.

There are numerous reality factors that affect this hypothetical model. One is the fact that the child who is nearest the bottom in academic performance is usually, but not always, the child who drops out. Research shows, however, that the school dropout generally drops from the lowest quarter of his class (Schreiber, 1966). Evans and Patrick (1969) reported that potential dropouts could be spotted as early as the fifth grade. The potential dropout has all of the characteristics that herald school failure. He is generally about a year older than his fifth-grade classmates, is in trouble academically, and is scoring significantly lower than his classmates on tests of academic achievement. In other words, he is already an old hand at meeting failure in the American school system.

Another reality factor that bears on the statistical model presented is regional variation in retention rates. Some areas of the country have much higher dropout rates than the national average, and some have much lower ones. For example, in a Texas community in which 80 per cent of the school children are Mexican Americans, 53 per cent of the fourth graders did not reach the twelfth grade (Carter, 1970). These children in a rural school with an extremely high dropout rate are *more* threatened than children in the suburban school, who—because of the lower dropout rate— are likely to maintain their relative positions throughout the school years.

In his 1965 message on education to Congress, President Lyndon Johnson observed, "In our fifteen largest cities, 60 per cent of the tenth-grade students from poverty neighborhoods drop out before finishing high school." The effects of this statistic are dramatic. Assuming again that it is the least successful students who drop out, students who were doing *above-average* work as sophomores in high school will—as a result of the dropout rate—graduate in the *bottom* third of their class. If senior high school teachers grade on the curve, a *B* student as a sophomore may quite suddenly find himself a *D* student as a senior—with *no* changes in his own study habits.

Even in suburban schools, where there is very little dropout and students tend to maintain their relative positions, to be in the top third of the class from first grade through high school represents something altogether different in our achievement-oriented society than to be forever in the lowest third. The psychology of failure is threatening and reinforcing.

The longitudinal growth study conducted by ETS provides an excellent opportunity to examine empirical data to see what actually happens to groups of students as they move from the seventh grade to the eleventh grade. Table 4 shows actual data collected from 633 students who scored in the lowest third of the eleventh-grade national norms in 1965 on the combined verbal and quantitative sections of the School and College Ability Tests (SCAT-T).

Starting with the top line, the data show that 100 per cent of the 633 students scored in the bottom third on SCAT-T in the eleventh grade, because that is the reference group with which we start. Thirty-four per cent of these same students, however, scored

Table 4. LOW-A ELEVENTH GRADERS SCORING IN HIGH, MIDDLE, AND LOW THIRDS ON SEVENTH-, NINTH-, AND ELEVENTH-GRADE NORMS

		Lowest Third	Middle Third	Highest Third
		Per Cent	*Per Cent*	*Per Cent*
1965	Eleventh Grade	100	0	0
1963	Ninth Grade	63	34	3
1961	Seventh Grade	52	45	3

Source: ETS Growth Study data.

in the *middle* third of national ninth-grade norms in 1963; and 45 per cent, or nearly half, were middle-third students relative to seventh graders across the country in 1961. In other words, nearly half of the young people in the Growth Study sample who made it to the eleventh grade but were fairly poor (lowest-third) students by the time they did so had been average (middle-third) students as seventh graders. Their route over five very important developmental years was downward. The other half of the unsuccessful students in the eleventh-grade class started their bout with failure even earlier; they were bottom-third students in the seventh grade. (The 3 per cent of the students scoring in the top third in the seventh and ninth grades probably represent measurement errors of the testing or unusual personal situations.)

The empirical data for the *top*-third students, shown in Table 5, look quite different. Of 1,721 students who scored in the top third on SCAT-T norms when they were in the eleventh grade in 1965, most had been in the top third all the way through school. None was ever in the bottom third. Some moved from the middle third to the top third. Thus, even with errors of measurement, the empirical data support the theoretical model that posits that top-third students sail through school with their relative position unassailed while their less facile classmates wage a perpetual battle to keep from slipping relatively lower as they proceed through school.

Table 5. HIGH-A ELEVENTH GRADERS SCORING IN HIGH, MIDDLE, AND LOW THIRDS ON SEVENTH-, NINTH-, AND ELEVENTH-GRADE NORMS

		Lowest Third	Middle Third	Highest Third
		Per Cent	*Per Cent*	*Per Cent*
1965	Eleventh Grade	0	0	100
1963	Ninth Grade	0	5	95
1961	Seventh Grade	0	12	87

Source: ETS Growth Study data.

SCOPE data show the toll taken in this battle. Thirty-eight per cent of the high school seniors who scored in the lowest third admitted that they often feel nervous, tense, or shy in class—as compared to 21 per cent of the high-A students; girls at all levels of ability expressed greater strain than boys. Holt (1970) presents a colorful description of the anxiety present in most American classrooms. When he asked elementary school children how they felt when the teacher asked them a question and they didn't know the answer, one boy "spoke for everyone" when he said in a loud voice, "Gulp!" "I asked them why they felt gulpish," wrote Holt. "They said they were afraid of failing, afraid of being kept back, afraid of being called stupid, afraid of feeling themselves stupid. Stupid. Why is it such a deadly insult to these children, almost the worst thing they can think of to call each other? Where do they learn this?" (p. 63).

One of the unintentional lessons learned by low-A students is that failure is always reaching out to envelop them. The picture is not unlike that of a strong and a weak swimmer thrown into downstream currents above a waterfall. The strong swimmer soon swims to calm waters and begins to focus his attention on how fast he can swim, while the weak swimmer is dragged into such swift currents that his only concern is to keep himself from going over the waterfall. In the language of psychology, the strong swimmer becomes achievement-motivated while the weak swimmer becomes fear-threatened. Future learning is structured differently for the two swimmers.

Atkinson and Feather (1966), in their theory of achievement motivation, point out that the typical achievement-oriented person works hardest at a task of intermediate difficulty, where his chances of success are 50-50. He is not challenged by a too-easy task because its successful completion is assured and hence will give him no rewarding feeling of success; neither does he choose a task in which his chances of success are quite slight, for in that case his reward is too unlikely. He is basically realistic, raising his aspirations with success and lowering them with failure. When he approaches a task where the outcome is ambiguous, he is motivated to try his skills because his past "batting average" allows him to predict success in a new venture even when relatively little concrete information is available concerning his chances. In other words, he has self-confidence and is willing to take some risks.

The Atkinson-Feather theory makes a different prediction, however, for the failure-threatened personality. If the major concern is to avoid failure, then the task of intermediate difficulty is to be shunned as most dangerous. The failure-threatened individual avoids tasks in which the outcome is uncertain. He is motivated to defend himself against the threat of failure either by selecting easy tasks, where success is virtually assured, or by attempting such difficult tasks that failure is expected and therefore not threatening. John Holt (1970) is a sensitive observer of children and his very readable book, *How Children Fail*, gives some insight into the experience of failure as it is lived daily by school children across the country. He observes, "Children [who fear failure] . . . may decide that if they can't have total success, their next best bet is to have total failure" (p. 85). That is exactly what Atkinson and Feather are saying in more complex and theoretical language.

This fear-of-failure reaction to learning may account for the highly unrealistic aspirations that many community college educators see in their low-ability students. Not to succeed at being a doctor or a lawyer is not very threatening, because neither the student nor his associates have any real expectation that such a goal will be realized. Froomkin's (1970) presentation of data showing that nearly one third of minority youth with "very low" scores on verbal-ability tests hoped to graduate from a four-year college lends support to the theory. Since fewer Caucasians of the same low level of tested ability (15 per cent) showed what must be labeled "unrealistically" high educational aspirations, the following explanation might be advanced. Some low-ability whites in the higher income brackets might "realistically" be expected, by themselves and by others, to graduate from college; therefore, since they might be called upon to prove that they could accomplish their goal, they are unlikely to expose themselves to that 50-50 area of risk by saying that they hoped to obtain a bachelor's degree. For a low-ability black youth to say that he plans to graduate from a four-year college represents a rather different situation. It is not threatening because, in the present society, he does not really expect to have the chance to prove whether he can or not; for him the possibility of a college degree is not 50-50.

The Coleman report (1966) attributed the differences in aspirations between low-scoring majority and minority youth to the lack of opportunity for minority youth to evaluate their performance realistically. Many low-scoring minority youth actually believe that they do fairly well in school because they evaluate their performance against that of their own schoolmates. Since they perform well by the standards of their own school, they have a higher self-regard than low-performing white children in suburban schools, which may offer comparison with a wider cross section of students.

There is no necessary conflict between the Coleman hypothesis and the fear-of-failure hypothesis advanced here. Coleman's explanation seems appropriate for upper-third students in ghetto schools (who may still score very low on national norms); the fear-of-failure explanation would fit those in the middle and lower thirds who find themselves dropping lower, relative to their classmates, as they proceed through school.

Aspirations need not be high to be unrealistic; fear-threatened personalities sometimes show very low aspirations. High school and community college teachers have observed students who doggedly repeat a lesson that they know while steadfastly refusing to venture to the next step in learning. These students have found that success is assured as long as they stick with something they know; failure threatens when they try new things. Theoretically, the explanation for low aspirations is that students can hardly be blamed for not accomplishing something that they do not attempt. They have learned to fear putting themselves to the test, and hence they do not get themselves involved in situations that involve the risk of failure. Holt (1970) has observed this characteristic in the learning approaches of children. He notes, "Incompetence has [an] advantage. Not only does it reduce what others expect and demand of you, it reduces what you expect or even hope for yourself. When you set out to fail, one thing is certain—you can't be disappointed. As the old saying goes, you can't fall out of bed when you sleep on the floor" (p. 86).

Experimental support for the fear-of-failure hypothesis can be found in the SCOPE data collected from high school seniors.

Students scoring in the lowest third on a test of academic ability were more than twice as likely as students scoring in the top third to want to avoid the possible "failure situation" of being rejected by a college of their choice. Forty-eight per cent of the low-A students and 21 per cent of the high-A students said, "If I were to apply to a college, I'd choose one I was sure of getting into." When students were asked whether they agreed or disagreed with the statement "I want to know that something will really work before I am willing to take a chance on it," 58 per cent of the low-A students and 37 per cent of the high-A students agreed that they wanted that assurance.

If these analyses are correct, we would predict that low-achieving, fear-threatened high school seniors would apply either to open-door community colleges or to highly selective colleges. They would be assured of acceptance at the open-door college, and to be turned down by Harvard is not really very threatening to the student who has no expectation of going there.

These theoretical and experimental analyses may have important implications for programs for the undereducated that are launched by moderately selective colleges such as many state colleges and universities. To students who have built their personality defenses to avoid failure, application for admission to these programs may prove very threatening indeed. The prestige of the colleges is not high enough to make rejection acceptable, nor are the standards low enough to make admission a certainty. For those students who do apply and are accepted, the college should be prepared to allocate adequate resources to provide the necessary instructional and counseling support while the fear-of-failure pattern is replaced with a more positive self-confident approach to learning.

A vivid example of what can happen when low-achieving students are accepted into a college that has no special provisions for help in reorienting their learning habits is illustrated by Rose (1965). She describes an experimental program that was tried and later abandoned by a state university. Although the university practiced nonselective admissions for in-state students, college officials felt that students with high school averages of less than C should be warned that their statistical chances of success were low. The 290 students falling in the high-risk category were sent a letter by the admissions office suggesting that academic difficulties could be expected and that, if the students still wished to enter, an interview was required. The interview, as described by Rose, certainly should have reinforced any fear-of-failure tendencies on the part of the students. But the counselor also gave advice about study habits, the necessity of carrying a light course load, the inadvisability of working part time, and the advisability of seeking help from the counseling service. The amazing thing is that only 10 per cent of those who came for the interview were discouraged by it. This situation could be accounted for by the fear-of-failure theory. The realization that aspirations are unrealistic will affect achievement-oriented personalities, but this would not be expected to affect failure-threatened personalities; and no doubt most of the students required to appear for the interview were failure-threatened. At the end of the first semester, 81 per cent of the group that had entered the college despite the warnings were on probation or had withdrawn. By the end of the second semester, only 8 per cent of the students were in good standing, compared with 41 per cent of the total freshman class, which served as the control group.

State universities with escalating academic standards frequently found themselves in this situation in the 1950s and early 1960s, and many attempted to deal with the problem in the manner described—by advising poor risks of the improbability of success. The author participated in one such effort as a member of the counseling staff at a state university wherein we were attempting to be realistic with lower-quarter students. To our amazement, we found that the best of the lowest-quarter students (for whom the choice was not totally unrealistic) "got the message" and withdrew, whereas the students with the poorest chances insisted on enrolling.

Today, the approach to low-achieving students is to admit them as high risks and to provide special programs for them. Many programs are claiming great success in retention, but there is not as yet much evidence of academic success as measured by college grades or tests of academic achievement.

According to the theoretical and research analyses just presented, successful remediation programs would need to devote considerable attention to a total reorientation of the students' approach to learning situations. The fairly successful College Discovery Program, launched by the City University of New York in 1965, has reported that after four semesters 57 per cent of the students were still enrolled (Tormes, 1969). Significantly, the major personal change attributed to the college experience by survivors in this program was an increase in self-confidence; among dropouts the major change was thought to be "a broadening of intellectual and career horizons." The fact that it was the survivors who reported increased self-confidence suggests that survivors changed their attitude toward learning, whereas dropouts simply checked a response that may have "sounded good" to them.

Holding unrealistic aspirations is one way of reacting to threats of failure. More troublesome to college personnel attempting to teach remedial courses is students' apparent passivity in learning situations. Students seem to be saying that they cannot fail at what they do not try. Instead of assuming that effort and success are related, the failure-threatened individual assumes that effort and failure are directly related.

In response to a questionnaire item (Appendix C) asking administrators of remedial services in two-year colleges what they perceived to be the *major obstacle* to learning for low-achieving students, "lack of effort, has quit trying" ranked first. The rankings in order of priority were as follows: (1) lack of effort, has quit trying; (2) poor home background; (3) poor elementary and secondary schooling; (4) fear of failure; (5) more interested in nonacademic matters such as car, sports, job; (6) the necessity of a job prevents time and energy for study; (7) low intelligence.

Some basic research in psychology has implications for understanding the phenomenon of passivity in learning. Seligman (1969) and his colleagues made laboratory dogs "passive" to new learning experiences and then experimented with procedures that would make them into "active" learners again. In a sense this is our goal for New Students—to take students whose natural curiosity and bent for learning have been stifled through past experiences with education and make them want to learn again. Although dogs are not people, the parallels to human learning and to failure-threatened personalities make for fascinating speculation and the generation of some testable hypotheses. Seligman and his colleagues conducted a standard conditioning experiment. Their naïve dogs behaved just as the dogs in the Psychology 100 textbooks do. In these experiments, the dog was placed in a box with an electric grid on the floor. The lights dimmed, ten seconds later the shock came on, and the dog howled and ran around showing fear and lack of purposive behavior. During this random activity, the dog managed to throw himself over the barrier and out of the box, at which point he escaped from shock and the lights went on again. The next time the lights dimmed, the dog started his fear reaction, the shock came on, and the escape from the box and the shock was more rapid and purposeful than before. With repeated trials, the dog finally jumped over the barrier as soon as the lights dimmed, thus avoiding the shock altogether.

But Seligman found that the reaction was very different for dogs who had previously been shocked in the box *while in a harness* that prevented escape. Twenty-four hours later, these dogs entered the conditioning experiment "knowing" that nothing they did would terminate the shock. Struggling in the harness had no effect. When they were later put in the box *unharnessed* and free to learn to escape just as the naïve dogs had been, they howled for just a few seconds when the shock came on and then settled down and took the shock. After several trials, the dogs ceased even to try to escape and became passive or helpless.

The situation is analogous to that of a young student who tries hard in the beginning but who finds that he never gets rewarded by an *A,* the teacher's approval, or classmates' admiration. In other words, his efforts, like those of the dog struggling in the harness, are futile. After repeated experience, he does learn something—that the result of trying is failure. The resultant personality characteristic would appear to be passivity in learning.

There is tentative research evidence that the phenomenon of passivity does exist among low-A students. On an active-passive scale used in the SCOPE questionnaire, low-A students tended to score lower (were more passive) than high-A students. The scale consisted of items such as "When I can't do something easily, I usually give up" and "When I face a tough problem, I don't work on it much because I probably won't solve it." Students scoring in the lowest third on the academic-ability measure were roughly twice as likely to exhibit traits of passivity as were high-A students. Forty-six per cent of the New Students and only 25 per cent of the traditional students scored in the lowest third of the high school seniors in the SCOPE sample.

The passivity of some of the high-risk students in the College Discovery Program at the City University of New York (CUNY) is illustrated by the finding that dropouts from the program studied fewer hours per week than survivors; furthermore, they were aware that they were studying less (Tormes, 1969). Other researchers also have commented on the passivity of low achievers (Roth and Meyersburg, 1963).

Clearly, new approaches to learning for these passive students must be found. The problem appears twofold: (1) how to restructure the learning situation so that they will try again and (2) how to reward the effort. Seligman worked with these same two problems when he tried to get his dogs to unlearn fatalistic acceptance and to learn that they could make responses to control the shock. After the dogs had quit trying to escape, they were not likely to leap over the barrier accidentally and thereby discover that they could avoid the shock. So Seligman set about the teaching task of showing helpless dogs that there could be a relationship between their responses and the termination of the shock: "We dropped meat on the other side of the barrier to encourage helpless dogs to escape shock; we took the barrier out altogether; we called to the dogs from the nonelectric side. Nothing worked. As a last resort, we pulled them back and forth across the box on leashes, forcibly demonstrating to them that movement in a certain direction ended shocks. This did the trick, but only after much dragging. Dogs so treated finally learned to escape shock on their own" (p. 44).

There is more than a little speculation involved in the assumption that animal learning is directly transferable to human behavior. Complex human learning is not *explained* by simple animal learning, but the conditioning experiments do permit some important observations by revealing with stark simplicity some of the elements of learning. The dogs in Seligman's experiment had "learned" that effort was futile, and it took a great deal of persuasion to convince them that the situation had changed and that they could exercise some control over what happened to them.

The analogy in human learning is this: The student who has

become passive must be shown that a new kind of learning situation exists—a situation in which he can almost certainly succeed if he makes an effort to do so. The "guaranteed-success" programs now being tried in some remedial-education programs show considerable promise for helping students to reorient themselves to learning tasks. (See Chapter 10 for a discussion of guaranteed-success programs and reorientation-to-learning courses for New Students.) The basic goal of guaranteed-success programs is in keeping with the Atkinson-Feather theory, which posits that failure-threatened personalities will approach tasks that are assured of success. The Seligman experiments indicate, however, that considerable persuasion and understanding and perhaps firmness may be necessary before the learner will take the initial steps that will show him that through his own efforts he can succeed in school learning tasks.

In summary, the research shows that the great majority of students who graduate in the lowest third of the high school class (New Students) have either been in the bottom third of the class throughout their school years or have had the experience of moving ever lower in academic performance relative to their classmates. Such experiences are extremely threatening to the self-esteem of young people; and New Students, as a result of their constant battle with failure in the school situation, are more fearful of putting their abilities to a test than are their more successful peers. They have learned that learning involves risks to the ego. There is, after all, always the chance that in approaching any new situation—which is the essence of learning—they might fail. Whereas the past experience of good students tells them that they probably will succeed, the past experience of poor students tells them that they will probably fail.

According to theory, one set of expectations results in achievement-oriented personalities whereas the other results in failure-threatened personalities. Successful students are motivated to try; unsuccessful students are motivated to protect themselves against the threat of failure by not trying. They seem to say, "If I don't try very hard, I can't fail very much."

The attitudes of New Students support the theory. They are less confident of their abilities; they avoid risk situations where possible; and they are more likely than traditional students to obtain passive scores on a scale measuring the tendency toward active or passive approaches to life and its demands. For New Students, the school situation has been a fearful experience, and the lessons they have learned are handicaps to future learning. In developing new educational programs for New Students, educators will first of all have to provide a new perception of the learning process.

References

ATKINSON, J. W., AND N. T. FEATHER. *A Theory of Achievement Motivation.* New York: John Wiley & Sons, 1966.

CARTER, T. P. *Mexican Americans in School: A History of Neglect.* New York: College Entrance Examination Board, 1970.

COLEMAN, J., ET AL. *Equality of Educational Opportunities.* Washington, D.C.: Government Printing Office, 1966.

EVANS, F., AND C. PATRICK. *Antecedents and Patterns of Academic Growth of School Dropouts.* Research Bulletin RB-69-81. Princeton: Educational Testing Service, 1969.

FROOMKIN, J. *Aspirations, Enrollments, and Resources.* Prepared for U.S. Office of Education. Washington, D.C.: Government Printing Office, 1970.

HOLT, J. *How Children Fail.* New York: Dell, 1970.

ROSE, H. A. "The Effect of Preadmission Interview on Students of Doubtful Academic Ability." *College and University Bulletin,* 1965, *41* (1), 80–88.

ROTH, R. M., AND H. A. MEYERSBURG. "The Non-Achievement Syndrome." *Personnel and Guidance Journal,* 1963, *41* (6), 535–540.

SCHREIBER, D. "Profile of the Dropout." In *The Disadvantaged Poor: Education and Employment.* Third Report of the Task Force on Economic Growth and Opportunity. Washington, D.C.: U.S. Chamber of Commerce, 1966.

SELIGMAN, M. E. P. "Can We Immunize the Weak?" *Psychology Today,* 1969, *3* (1), 42.

TORMES, Y. M., ed. "Some Differences in Dropouts and Survivors in the College Discovery Program." *Research Briefs.* New York: City University of New York, 1969.

HOME AND SCHOOL: SHARPES OF ATTITUDES

3

The past home and school experiences of young people have a profound effect upon the formation of attitudes and values. As we have seen, New Students have had different school experiences from those of traditional students. New Students have also been exposed to very different home environments. Almost two thirds of the New Students as they are defined in this book are the children of blue-collar workers who ceased formal education upon graduation from high school or earlier (Appendix B).

In his book *Whitetown USA* Binzen (1970) reports on a study of predominantly white blue-collar communities. He writes of the fierce pride, the alienation, and the "white rage" that simmers in the blue-collar industrial fringes of our cities. Despite the fact that these communities are 99.7 per cent white, young people growing up in these environments have much in common with black youth from the inner city. They do almost as badly on tests of academic achievement, and the attitudes of Whitetown and Blacktown parents are conservative and almost identical: most favor Bible-reading in school, tough discipline, and conventional behavior.

Because both parental attitudes and school experiences affect student attitudes about education, about self, and about life, an examination of some differences between subgroups of New Students to higher education may help in understanding the attitudes and values of New Students. To provide perspective, we shall look first at the broad constellation of attitudes and values that differentiate the personality characteristics of New Students (as low A's) from traditional students (as high A's). Then we shall compare attitudes about education as they appear in more complex groupings, such as blue-collar high A's with blue-collar low A's. And finally, we will look at the attitudes of two subgroups of New Students—those who have been successful in school despite test scores that predicted poor performance and those for whom the tests were more accurate indicators of school performance.

Personality Characteristics

The attitudes and values that are learned as young people interact with their environments contribute to the formation of what we popularly call the personality of the individual. Most of us, consciously or subconsciously, stereotype people to try to get a rapid impression of how they will think and behave. Rightly or wrongly, we expect a "long-haired hippie type" to think and act differently from a "clean-shaven hard-hat type." Experience proves us right frequently enough to maintain the stereotype. Stereotyping on the basis of dress—over which the individual has some element of control—will probably be more accurate than stereotyping on the basis of something the individual cannot determine. We are often mistaken, for example, if we expect a particular woman to be dependent and interested in children, or if we expect an older person to be conservative and oriented to the past, or if we expect a black to speak non-standard English or to be militant. New Students, as defined in this book, tend not to have been successful in traditional school activities, and they are predominantly from the homes of blue-collar workers. Those two facts alone conjure up some images about their personalities—about how they will think and behave. How correct are those stereotypes?

Data from the SCOPE study provide a research picture of some personality characteristics of New Students compared with those of traditional students. The descriptions cannot be used, of course, to stereotype individual New Students. Some will fit the general pattern; others will not.

The SCOPE staff built upon the work that the Center for Research and Development in Higher Education of the University of California, Berkeley, had done in studying the attitudes and values of college students. The Omnibus Personality Inventory (Heist and Yonge, 1968) was designed to study the personality characteristics of normal college students, with special emphasis on academic and intellectual activities. Using as a foundation the Omnibus Personality Inventory (OPI), the SCOPE staff developed six scales that have special relevance for the study of New Students. I then used the SCOPE data to look at the ways in which the attitudes and values of New Students differ from those of traditional students on the personality scales.

One stereotype that we have about blue-collar workers is that they tend to be politically conservative and wish to preserve the authority that has been traditionally exercised by social institutions. As measured by the Autonomy Scale, New Students fit this stereotype of blue-collar workers. Youth who score high on Autonomy tend to be liberal, nonauthoritarian, tolerant of viewpoints different from their own, and nonjudgmental in their relationships with people. The differences between low-A and high-A students on this scale are dramatic. Over half (58 per cent) of the low A's scored in the lowest third on the scale (authoritarian), with only 13 per cent scoring in the top third. Scores for the high A's were just the other way around; 54 per cent scored in the top third, with 15 per cent scoring low. In some ways, it seems puzzling that the have-nots—and surely low-SES and low-ability students are have-nots—should be endorsing statements on the Autonomy Scale that read, "People ought to be satisfied with what they have" or "Every wage earner should be required to save a certain part of his salary each month so that he will be able to support himself and his family in later years." But these attitudes are consistent with what used to be referred to as "staunch American independence." New Students do tend to agree with statements that make virtues of hard work, determination, and ambition; and they tend not to respect those who think such qualities old-fashioned. Many politically conservative people who deplore the egalitarian spread of higher education would feel much happier if they realized that the New Students now attending egalitarian institutions of higher education actually reflect their own attitudes. For example, 66 per cent of the New Students agree that "More than anything else, it is good hard work that makes life worthwhile," while only 42 per cent of the traditional students accept the statement as true. New Students tend to respect the traditional institutions of church, school, and government. Past research has been in agreement in finding that the authoritarian values illustrated by unquestioning acceptance of authority are consistently related to lower ability, lower educational achievement, and lower socioeconomic status. New Students are very much a product of their blue-collar backgrounds when contrasted with the more liberal, critical traditional students, who show an increasing unwillingness to accept establishment values. (See Adorno et al. for a full discussion of authoritarianism.)

The scores of New Students on the OPI scale entitled Theoretical Orientation (TO) are also predictably lower than those of traditional students. The TO Scale is intended to measure a preference for logical, analytical, and critical thinking of the type used in scientific work. The items also seem to measure the student's interest in intellectual problem-solving as an activity. Many teachers working with both low-A and high-A students could predict the direction of answers to the item "I prefer to have a problem explained to me rather than trying to figure it out myself." Forty per cent of the low A's and 19 per cent of the high A's agree with the statement. New Students, with their lower self-confidence in intellectual tasks, are more eager for assistance than are high-A students, who may enjoy the challenge of intellectual problem-solving. Another item on the TO scale has special significance for teaching low-A students. High-A students are twice as likely as low-A students (41 per cent to 21 per cent) to prefer a "long complicated problem to several shorter ones."

The items of the TO scale seem relevant to the theory of achievement discussed in Chapter 2. According to that theory, achievement-oriented personalities are interested in the learning process itself. They tend to be internally motivated to figure things out for themselves and to want to accomplish a task because its completion will result in personal satisfaction. Failure-threatened personalities, on the other hand, tend to focus on "getting the answer," so that they will *look* successful. They prefer having things explained to them because it seems a more certain path to the correct answer, and frequent signposts along the way bolster self-confidence and assure them that they are on the correct path. Their desire to avoid risky situations that might result in failure is further illustrated by their endorsement of the statement "I want to know that something will really work before I am willing to take a chance on it." Fifty-eight per cent of the low A's and 37 per cent of the high A's agreed. The Theoretical Orientation Scale, which seems to probe the general dimension of intellectual self-confidence, shows 47 per cent of the New Students and 22 per cent of the traditional students scoring in the lowest third among the high school seniors in the SCOPE sample.

The OPI Scale entitled Thinking Introversion (TI), modi-fied by SCOPE, shows less difference between traditional and New Students than might be predicted. High scores on TI indicate that the student has said he enjoys literature and the arts and finds plea-sure in working with ideas. Low scorers tend to like overt action and to consider ideas worthwhile only if they have practical applications. Although a larger percentage of low-A students than high-A students score in the lower third on TI (41 per cent to 31 per cent), the difference is no greater than that between males and females (44 per cent to 32 per cent). Three of the nine items on the TI Scale are related to music and the preference for popular or classical music; and none of the items seem to test the preferences that we might predict would have special relevance for us in our study of New Students—items, for instance, on preference for the physical, action-oriented mode of learning that is said to be useful with younger disadvantaged children (Riessman, 1962), or items assess-ing preference for practical, pragmatic tasks that emphasize the *uses* of ideas instead of the *manipulation* of ideas.

Two other scales developed by the SCOPE staff are of special interest in describing New Students. Considerable attention has been given in the literature to the presumed inability of disad-vantaged students to delay gratification or to work for a reward that is not immediate. The Deferment of Satisfaction Scale (DS) does differentiate between low-A and high-A students in this respect.

Thirty-eight per cent of the low-A students scored in the lowest third on DS, compared to only 16 per cent of the high-A students. While girls generally indicated more willingness than boys to plan for future satisfaction, the differences were especially apparent in the low-A group. Whereas nearly half (48 per cent) of the low-A males scored in the lowest third on the DS scale, less than a third (31 per cent) of the low-A women did.

It is perhaps ironic that one of the most eagerly accepted innovations in community colleges is the deemphasis on grades. About three out of ten (27 per cent) of the community colleges say they have adopted some variant of nonpunitive grading (see Appendix C). Certainly this reform is consistent with recommendations that would arise from an analysis of the failure experience presented in Chapter 2. But there are other considerations. Grades are concrete rewards for effort expended and, as we shall see later, are more important to New Students than to traditional students. Most of the colleges where the effects of a deemphasis on grades have been studied carefully are elite colleges working with a very different type of student than those of concern here. After a comprehensive review of the literature, Warren (1971) concluded: "The motivating effect of grades is complex and not well understood. Some students value the formal affirmation of accomplishment that grades represent and work to get it. For others, the almost continual self-assessment derived from cues provided by teachers, other students and regular course activities is sufficient" (p. 14).

It is not yet clear what effect the practice of grading has on the learning of New Students. It does seem clear that some form of evaluative feedback should be provided. Perhaps the ideal solution would be to find concrete symbols of individual accomplishment that are noncompetitive and immediate. Those concerned with criterion-referenced testing are pursuing this line of reasoning. Further attention is given to the subject within the context of the proposals suggested in Chapter 10.

The Active-Passive Scale (AP) used in the SCOPE study attempted to distinguish between people who actively pursue what they want versus those who passively accept what they get. Low A's tended to be passive; 46 per cent of them scored in the lowest third, compared with 25 per cent of the high A's. Of some interest is the finding that very few people—low A or high A—admit that they usually give up when they cannot do something easily; 80 per cent of the low A's and 84 per cent of the high A's claimed that they usually keep trying. Large differences between low A's and high A's occurred in a question asking how venturesome they would be in seeking college admission. Girls were more willing to risk being turned down by the college of their choice than boys; but high-A students (82 per cent of the girls and 75 per cent of the boys) were much more likely than low-A students (54 per cent of the girls and 47 per cent of the boys) to say that they would apply to a college they really wanted to attend even if their chances for admission were uncertain. In this particular case, however, it is important to remember that lowest-third students do not have a very good chance of getting into any college that is selective. Their fear of being turned down by a college where their chances for admission are uncertain is based on reality.

Finally, an OPI Scale that has had great usefulness with traditional college students is a complex, multifaceted scale entitled Intellectual Disposition (ID). In the SCOPE study it consisted of a combination of items from the Au, TI, and TO Scales. Intellectual Disposition classifies respondents along a continuum representing intellectual-scholarly interests. Heist and Yonge (1968) describe it as a measure of the "potential for behaving intellectually." If the thesis that the meritocratic model of academic excellence is not appropriate for New Students is correct, New Students should score significantly lower on ID than traditional students. And they do. Fifty-five per cent of the low-A students score in the lowest third on ID, compared with only 16 per cent of high-A students; similarly, 59 per cent of the traditional students score in the top third, compared with only 16 per cent of the New Students.

The two scales that distinguish New Students from traditional students most sharply are Autonomy (independence of thought and judgment and general nonauthoritarian attitudes) and Intellectual Disposition (interest in intellectual, scholarly activities). In the rough analyses performed here, the simple fifteen-item Autonomy Scale does as good a job of differentiating between the values of traditional and New Students as does the longer Intellectual Disposition Scale (thirty-one items). Interestingly enough, the Autonomy Scale is the only one of the six scales described here that contains *no* item related directly to school work or to study habits. It is strictly a scale of cultural attitudes, and on it New Students appear to hold the attitudes around which the town-gown polarization has developed, with New Students espousing the attitudes of the community as opposed to those of faculty and students on traditional campuses. Some of the attitudes which traditional students have vociferously disavowed are held by substantial numbers of New Students. Examples of some of these items from the Au Scale are "I am in favor of strict enforcement of laws no matter what"; "Communism is the most hateful thing in the world today"; and "It is never right to disobey the government." Research is virtually unanimous in reporting that the greatest attitude changes to take place among students attending college occur along the dimension of Authoritarianism. If this becomes the case for New Students, then the country may experience an "education gap" between New Students and their relatively poorly educated parents that is much greater than the much-discussed "generation gap" (Cross, 1967; Fields, 1971).

Different Home Environments

Data from the Comparative Guidance and Placement Program (CGP) offered an opportunity to look at the attitudes of more complex groupings of New Students than those based upon the broad categories of low A and high A. By establishing four groups of students, we could look at similarities and differences in the attitudes of students with similar home backgrounds but different school experiences and vice versa. It was possible to classify 9,490 CGP students who were entering community colleges in the fall of 1969 into four groups. Group 1 consisted of low-SES New Students—students who scored in the lowest one third (low A) of the total CGP sample on a traditional verbal test (see Appendix A) and whose fathers were blue-collar workers.[1] Group 2 consisted of low-A

[1] Unskilled, semiskilled, skilled, or service workers are considered blue-collar workers; white-collar workers include those in professions that require a bachelor's degree or more, or executive status. Middle-level status, including salesmen, office workers, junior executives, and managers, is excluded from these groupings.

students with high-status white-collar fathers. Group 3 consisted of high-scoring (top-third) students with blue-collar fathers; and group 4 consisted of the high-achieving sons and daughters of white-collar fathers. Table 6 shows how the 9,490 students were distributed.

Table 6. ENTERING TWO-YEAR-COLLEGE STUDENTS
BY VERBAL APTITUDE AND FATHERS' OCCUPATIONS

Fathers' Occupations	Verbal Test Score		
	Lowest Third	Highest Third	Total
Blue Collar	(1) 4,796	(3) 2,925	7,721
White Collar	(2) 692	(4) 1,077	1,769
Total	5,488	4,002	9,490

Source: CGP, 1969.

Students in group 1 possess the home and school backgrounds that we think of as most typical of New Students. They are doubly disadvantaged, coming as they do from homes of low socioeconomic status and doing poor work in school. Numerically they represent the largest of the four subgroups, with about half of the total group falling in this category. This group also contained the heaviest concentration of non-Caucasian students; 81 per cent of the students of ethnic minority backgrounds fell in this doubly disadvantaged category. An analysis of the non-Caucasian groups showed that very few of the 2,350 non-Caucasians in the CGP sample escaped the double handicap of low SES and low A. Only 26 minority students (1 per cent) fell in the privileged group of high SES and high A. Twelve per cent (292 minority students) could be described as upwardly mobile through education; these students came from the homes of blue-collar workers but were high achievers in school, ranking in the top third of the CGP sample of community college entrants. Five per cent (123 students) of the minority students were from the homes of college-educated fathers doing professional work, but the students themselves scored low on the criterion test.

Returning to the total sample of 9,490 students, we see that group 3 (high-ability sons and daughters of blue-collar workers) is the second largest in size, with 2,925 students (about one third of the total sample). These students represent the most upwardly mobile segment of the community college population. The majority are enrolled in the transfer curriculum of the community college, and most will go on to a bachelor's degree. Their primary need is probably financial assistance. On the basis of these rough indices, they possess both the ability and the motivation to succeed in the traditional college curriculum.

Group 2 (high SES and low A) is the smallest group, with 692 (7 per cent) of the students. These students will probably take jobs of lesser academic qualifications than those held by their fathers —although some of them will graduate from nonselective four-year colleges.

Group 4 is the group that we have referred to as traditional college students. Although these high-SES–high-A students represent only 11 per cent of this two-year-college sample, they might constitute 90 to 95 per cent of the student body of a selective university. One might inquire about the motivations of these students, who presumably have both the ability and the financial resources to start their college study in a four-year institution. Many of them are women who may be preparing to become nurses or secretaries; others may be residents of states where most students begin their college careers in junior colleges. With the rapid expansion of the purposes of junior colleges, there are any number of personal reasons why students might choose to begin their college careers in the two-year college. Some motivations may become apparent as we examine the data presented in Tables 7 through 12.

Table 7 shows the percentage of each of the four subgroups planning to pursue college-parallel curricula in college. Most students with high test scores plan to continue with more of the traditional education at which they have excelled in the past. New Students (low A's) of either high or low SES are more likely to be found in the technical or vocational curricula of two-year colleges.

Notice that low-A blue-collar students are the only group to have a majority enrolled in programs other than the traditional college-parallel course of study. Remember, too, that this is the largest of the four subgroups represented in the CGP sample. The primary

Table 7. ENTERING TWO-YEAR-COLLEGE STUDENTS
IN COLLEGE-PARALLEL CURRICULUM

	Percentage
High A, White Collar	76
High A, Blue Collar	65
Low A, White Collar	57
Low A, Blue Collar	43

Source: CGP, 1969.

influence in choice of curriculum is *academic* ability. Students scoring high on the test, regardless of the occupation of their fathers, tend to elect the traditional college-parallel option. *Within* a given range of ability, however, a student is more likely to choose the college-parallel course of study if his father is a white-collar worker.

There is a tendency for children to follow in the occupational footsteps of their fathers. If the low-A and high-A children of white-collar fathers are considered as a single group (not shown in Table 7), 69 per cent of the white-collar students are pursuing the college-parallel curriculum and probably plan to enter an occupational level similar to that of their fathers; 49 per cent of the total group of blue-collar students are preparing for blue-collar vocations. A significant number of high-A children of blue-collar fathers (1,901 in this sample), however, will strive for upward mobility through education; and a small group (298) of low-A children of white-collar fathers will probably settle for a lower occupational status than that of their parents. Overall, it appears that about one third (31 per cent) of the youth from white-collar professional homes attending community colleges are preparing for occupations requiring *less* education than their fathers had, while over half (51 per cent) of the blue-collar youth hope to move up to occupations requiring more education than their fathers had.

There is some evidence that the desire to move up the educational ladder is more than mere wish on the part of blue-collar youth attending two-year colleges. Table 8 shows the percentage in each subgroup saying that school grades are either very important or quite important to them.

Table 8. ENTERING TWO-YEAR-COLLEGE STUDENTS
SAYING GRADES ARE IMPORTANT

	Percentage
Low A, Blue Collar	84
Low A, White Collar	75
High A, Blue Collar	74
High A, White Collar	65

Source: CGP, 1969.

Grades, the symbols of achievement for young people whose chief business is going to school, are most important to those who have the hardest time getting them. And perhaps that is to be expected. The size of the percentages shows that grades are considered important by most young people; but for some borderline students they will become crucial gateways to futures, determining whether the student passes a course, remains in school, or attains a degree. Within the blue-collar groups, low-A students are 10 per cent more likely than high-A students of the same general background to attach great importance to grades; and exactly the same differential exists between low-A and high-A students from white-collar homes. But for students of roughly equal ability, those from blue-collar backgrounds value grades more than do those with professional and executive fathers. This finding may reflect the importance of the credentialing function of education for upwardly mobile youth; good grades are quite realistically a way to get ahead. However, a theme that recurs throughout the data on attitudes and interests reveals the preference of low-A and/or low-SES youth for concrete tangible rewards as opposed to more implicit intangible rewards. Grades, the tangible symbols of accomplishment, are valued by 84 per cent of the young people who represent educationally and socioeconomically disadvantaged New Students to higher education.

Students from blue-collar homes are more likely than their white-collar peers to feel that grades are important; and, in a sample of students entering two-year colleges, they are also likely to have made better grades in high school. Table 9 shows the percentage of each group reporting that they had better than a *C* average in high school.

Table 9. ENTERING TWO-YEAR-COLLEGE STUDENTS
MAKING ABOVE A *C* AVERAGE IN HIGH SCHOOL

	Percentage
High A, Blue Collar	77
High A, White Collar	68
Low A, Blue Collar	54
Low A, White Collar	49

Source: CGP, 1969.

Of course, those who score high on a test known to predict grades would make better high school grades than low scorers, regardless of SES. But the finding that blue-collar youth markedly outperform white-collar youth of the same general band of ability seems a reversal of the usual trends. The explanation probably lies in the fact that the CGP sample represents only entrants to two-year colleges. Highly able academically oriented blue-collar youth may attend the two-year college because they lack the money to go elsewhere. In contrast, the children of the rather high-status white-collar parents used in these groupings probably did not choose the two-year college primarily for its low cost. As a group, their academic motivation may be low. They may be attending a community college because they want specialized training in a career field, because their friends are going there, because they want to live at home, or for any of a number of personal reasons that are not related to their motivation for academic study.

Table 10. ENTERING TWO-YEAR-COLLEGE STUDENTS
SCORING ABOVE THE MEAN ON VOCATIONAL MOTIVATION

	Percentage
Low A, Blue Collar	56
Low A, White Collar	46
High A, Blue Collar	41
High A, White Collar	34

Source: CGP, 1969.

Data in Table 10 show, moreover, that blue-collar youth have not only greater academic motivation but also greater motivation to achieve vocationally. The conclusion seems to be that highly motivated white-collar youth, without the financial restraints of their blue-collar fellow students, enter four-year institutions, whereas highly motivated blue-collar youth are found in substantial numbers in community colleges. Blue-collar students who are not well motivated for further education do not enter college at all, whereas white-collar youth of the same low motivation may simply take the path of least resistance and enter a college near home.

The Vocational Motivation Scale of the CGP attempts to assess the student's interest in a vocation and in particular his attitude about education as preparation for a career. It consists of items such as "The main reason for continuing your education beyond high school is to prepare for a job that pays well." Alternatives range from "strongly agree" to "strongly disagree." Another example: "In school this year, do you plan to concentrate mainly on learning things that will be useful to you in your future work?" The four possible responses range from "definitely yes" to "definitely no."

Low-A students are more likely than high-A students to view

education as a means to better jobs. But, significantly, attitudes about the purposes of education appear to be shaped more by experience in the school system than by family background. Low-A students are more vocationally oriented than high-A students regardless of home background. High-A students are not as concerned as low A's about the usefulness of education. When asked whether they planned to concentrate mainly on learning things that would be useful to them in their future work during their first year of college, 36 per cent of the low A's and 25 per cent of the high A's said "definitely yes." It should be recognized, however, that many of the low-A students had already entered college with the intention of preparing themselves for jobs. A nursing student, for example, is much more likely to associate college study with specific job skills than is a student pursuing a general liberal-arts curriculum. In support of this observation are data showing that low-A women pursuing nursing and business careers score especially high on the Vocational Motivation Scale of the CGP.

The data presented so far have all dealt, in one way or another, with aspects of students' attitudes about education—choice of curricula, importance assigned to grades, perceptions of the purpose of education, past record of school success. There is a common pattern emerging: young people's perceptions about education seem shaped more by their experiences in the school system than by their experiences at home. In Tables 7 through 10, all of the *primary* groupings are based on test scores, with *secondary* groupings deriving from father's occupation. Although the criteria for grouping used here are admittedly rough, as is the analysis, the hypothesis suggested is that, when it comes to attitudes and values about education, students are more likely to think like their academic-class peers than they are to think like their social-class peers.

In some areas, however, socioeconomic class plays a more important role than academic ability. Not surprisingly, those areas have to do with financial resources for education.

Table 11 shows the percentages of each subgroup saying that they planned to work more than fifteen hours per week during the school year. The order corresponds exactly to that shown by the Financial Need Indicator[2] of the CGP. The results are as expected:

[2] The Financial Need Indicator is an index derived from student

Table 11. ENTERING TWO-YEAR-COLLEGE STUDENTS
PLANNING TO WORK MORE THAN FIFTEEN HOURS PER WEEK
AND HAVING CONSIDERABLE FINANCIAL NEED

	Work More Than Fifteen Hours	Considerable Financial Need
	Per Cent	Per Cent
Low A, Blue Collar	52	71
High A, Blue Collar	45	62
Low A, White Collar	41	50
High A, White Collar	32	36

Source: CGP, 1969.

students from working-class families have greater financial need and plan to work longer hours during the school year than do those from the families of professionals. On the whole, the Financial Need Indicator separates the groups more sharply than do students' statements about plans to work. If there is any surprise in these data, it is found in the small (4 per cent) difference between the high-A, blue-collar group and the low-A, white-collar group who plan to work extensively during the school year. The probable explanation is that whereas the child of working-class parents may *have* to help with college expenses, the young person of low academic ability may work as a matter of preference—to find the satisfactions out of school that have not been forthcoming in school.

These analyses indicate that New Students are a product of both home and school environments. Those students who have experienced success (or lack of success) in traditional schools seem somewhat more likely to share common attitudes about education than do students from similar socioeconomic backgrounds. Since

answers to questions in the Biographical Inventory concerning family financial circumstances. If the family resources available for education total $625 or less for the year, the student is classified as having considerable need even at a low-cost institution. (For further details, see the CGP *Interpretive Manual, 1969–70.*)

school success appears strongly related to the attitudes that a student brings to postsecondary education, let us turn attention now to some New Students who have succeeded academically.

Attitudes of High-Achieving New Students

Recently, a great deal of attention has been given to the fact that some students succeed in college despite the predictions of test scores that say they will not. In this book, we have defined New Students as those who score low on a criterion test that is directly related to school grades. And we have frequently referred to New Students as a group for whom school learning has been an unhappy and frustrating experience. When New Students are considered *as a group,* these descriptions are valid; but there are individual New Students for whom the tests are inaccurate predictors. Some students who make low test scores do very well in school. Who are these students who do better school work than their test scores predict?

Of the 9,921 students who scored in the lowest third of the CGP sample on the criterion test, 1,308 (13 per cent) had made grades of *B* or better in high school. (College grades would have been preferable, but they were not available at the time of the analysis.) These 1,308 students are actually misclassified as New Students—both because they have apparently done well enough in school to avoid the failure experience previously described and because their grades would probably have made them eligible for college admission at many colleges even under meritocratic standards. For some unknown number of this group of students, the test score may have been low because of unusual personal circumstances; but the finding that, as a group, they have some characteristics in common deserves a closer look.

The discrepancy between test scores and achievement as measured by grades can be viewed either as underprediction on the part of the test or as overachievement on the part of the students. Among the traditional college population, researchers have been most interested in students who score well on tests but do not perform well in class—the underachievers. (See Kornrich, 1965, or Thorndike, 1963, for comprehensive discussions of underachievement.) When considering New Students, however, researchers have emphasized the phenomenon of test bias, which may exist when students who do poorly on tests perform adequately in college. (For discussions of this issue, see Kendrick, 1967–68, or Thomas and Stanley, 1969.)

Many factors can influence test scores, and tests are not infallible predictors for individuals. But low-A students who *have* been successful in school differ in some ways from those for whom test scores proved more accurate. The data in Table 12 represent responses of *only low-A students* to selected alternatives of some Biographical Inventory items of the CGP battery. There were 726 men and 582 women who scored in the bottom third on the test but who reported high school grade averages of *B* or better. Their responses to the questionnaire items are compared with those of the 6,215 men and 2,398 women who also scored in the lowest third on the test but for whom the tests indicated more accurately the level of their academic achievement; they reported high school averages below *B*.

Because of the large sample size, differences as small as 5 per cent approach statistical significance, but the differences that are educationally significant are the large discrepancies such as those occurring in items 1 and 2. In the data for both men and women, it is immediately apparent that, among students who make low test scores, those who say they study hard make better grades. The Academic Motivation Scale of the CGP separates high and low achievers to an even greater extent, and it looks promising in identifying a group of New Students who are likely to perform beyond expectations based on test scores alone. The Academic Motivation Scale consists of items such as "How many study skills did you learn in high school?" "Do you think you worked harder on your classroom assignments than most other students in your high school classes?" "How many of your high school teachers thought you were one of the hardest workers, whether or not you were one of the smartest ones in your class?" "When you were in high school, how often did you put off or fail to finish uninteresting homework assignments?" The attitudes toward education and, more broadly, the personality characteristics implied in positive responses to these questions correspond very well with much of the past research on overachievement and underachievement. Some work recently reported by Smith (1967) indicates that the accuracy of predicting high

Table 12. SELECTED RESPONSES OF NEW STUDENTS TO BIOGRAPHICAL INVENTORY ITEMS

	Males		Females	
Inventory Items	*B* Average and Better $N = 726$	Less than *B* Average $N = 6{,}215$	*B* Average and Better $N = 582$	Less than *B* Average $N = 2{,}398$
	Per Cent	*Per Cent*	*Per Cent*	*Per Cent*
1. Studied more than classmates as high school senior.	57	31	70	51
2. Above-average scores on Academic Motivation Scale of CGP.	66	32	82	53
3. Want help with study techniques.	70	76	74	80
4. Plan to work more than 15 hours per week.	54	69	38	35
5. Father skilled or unskilled worker.	72	65	73	72
6. Know exactly life work desired.	24	19	39	35
7. Education is mostly or entirely job training.	42	43	47	46
8. Above-average scores on Vocational Motivation Scale of CGP.	52	50	61	57
9. College-Parallel Curriculum.	51	48	35	33

Source: CGP, 1969.

school and college grades could be more than doubled by the addition of peer ratings of personality on such characteristics as responsibility, dependability, self-reliance, and persistence (*Behavior Today,* 1970).

Perhaps the most comprehensive study of the relationship between personality measures and school success has been reported by Project TALENT (Flanagan et al., 1964). In a massive assault on the question, the TALENT staff computed thousands of correlations among thirteen specially constructed measures of personality, twenty-one measures of cognitive functioning, twelve indices of study habits, and a variety of items related to the backgrounds and experiences of high school seniors.

As with most personality data, the correlations with school achievement were not high; but from those that are statistically significant we can construct the following generalized personality picture of students who make good grades in high school. They describe themselves as leaders and as calm, even-tempered, confident, and usually at ease. They maintain that they are hard-working and dependable and that they make good use of their time, turn out work rapidly, and do their job even when they don't feel like it. They value good manners and good taste and are neat in appearance and work habits. In school, they say, they have no trouble keeping their minds on their studies, are good readers, and have little trouble expressing themselves. They like difficult assignments and do a little more than the course requires. They direct their attention to important points and feel that they are productive and conscientious about keeping up with assignments.

It is no strain on credulity to believe that young people possessing these characteristics make good grades. The traits seem to cluster, and the very frequency with which they occur together has given rise to labels for the syndrome. In professional circles, the cluster may be termed the "achievement syndrome"; laymen are familiar with the "Protestant ethic," and most recently the phrase "middle-class values" has come into prominence. The latter term is used, often in a pejorative way, to describe students who behave in a manner pleasing to teachers—studying hard, handing in assignments on time, paying attention in class.

Personality characteristics such as conscentiousness, responsibility, and perseverance are easily observable. A seven-year study recently completed at Brown University and reported in *Education, U.S.A.* (1970) claimed that ratings made by high school counselors in the student's senior year in high school remained valid through graduate school. The experimenters concluded, "Students who have low measured ability but who present evidence of high academic achievement prior to admission—the overachievers—are good students to bet on." Apparently, a positive attitude and willingness and motivation to work hard on school work will compensate to some extent for low academic aptitude. The fact that overachievers are less desirous of help with study habits (item 3, Table 12) than are other low-A students is further evidence of the extent to which they feel they have marshalled their efforts to an effective degree.

The significant differences between high- and low-performance males on items 4 and 5 are of considerable interest. Males who did not make especially good grades in high school plan to spend *more* time on jobs during the school year than those who have better reason to think that they could afford the time away from studies. Furthermore, item 5 shows that the financial need of those planning more extensive work out of school is not the explanatory factor. The usual interpretation of the combination of poor grades with high number of hours of employment is that jobs interfere with studies. But this apparently obvious explanation involves the old questions of cause and effect. Does employment during the school year cause poor grades—or do poor grades cause the student to seek success outside of school? Students who find that frustration and feelings of inferiority are the usual result of competition at academic tasks may well seek their rewards elsewhere. The ability to perform well on the job, the feelings of independence, and the things that money will buy probably have a special appeal for the young person who is making poor grades.

If this is the case, it should be possible to make some statements regarding the relationship between hours spent working, extent of financial need, and school achievement. Maximum hours of work would take place under conditions of large financial need and low school achievement. Minimum hours of work would occur with low financial need and high grades. And either high financial need and high grades or low financial need and low grades should lead to intermediate loads of outside work. The high-need, high-grades group would be satisfying economic needs, whereas the low-need, low-grades group would be gratifying psychological needs.

At first glance, the statements appear not applicable to women. In fact, there seems to be little relationship between grades and jobs on items 4 and 5 for women. The above argument, however, is based upon the assumption that a job carries with it certain psychological rewards. This assumption, in all probability, is not nearly so valid for teen-age girls as it is for teen-age boys for a number of reasons. Whereas a job bespeaks adult status for boys, the more common symbol of adulthood for girls is marriage and a home. Jobs, especially after school and at night, are not easily available for girls, and those that are available require such low-level skills that there is little opportunity to demonstrate competence to peers or, indeed, even to oneself. And lastly, spending money does not carry the status for girls that it does for boys. A girl who has her own car, for example, is viewed quite differently from a boy who has a car. For all of these reasons, plus the fact that females seem to be more nearly working up to capacity than males at this age, the data seem consistent with the hypothesis.

Item 6 in Table 12 indicates that high achievers are a little more likely to have made a career choice than are low achievers. But there are no differences between low and high achievers on items 7, 8, and 9. Academic achievement and the willingness to work hard at it does not necessarily mean that high achievers are any more academically oriented than their low-achieving classmates. Apparently, low-A students who make good grades are hard workers, but they seem not to be dedicated scholars. Low-ability students who have been successful in school tend to view education in vocational terms just as do other New Students. This observation offers some support for the hypothesis that vocational interests are a positive choice for low-A students rather than the negative nonchoice that they are often assumed to be.

Data presented in this chapter indicate that New Students have a different orientation to school learning tasks than do traditional students. Given the considerable differences in their past learning experiences—at home and in school—these research results correspond to the observations of many teachers who have had years of experience working with New Students. But it is surprising how often these differences are ignored. There is a distressing tendency to think that educational reform is educational reform, and that what is good for some students is good for all students. Some innovative reformers in community colleges seem to recommend the same kinds of reforms as those recommended for senior colleges. But the things that need changing to make traditional education more appropriate for New Students are not necessarily those advocated by the elite colleges that frequently serve as the models for educational change. Community colleges and vocational and technical institutes need to develop their own breed of educational reformers.

At the present time, there is considerable debate over whether to emphasize changing the schools or whether to work on modifying the behavior of unsuccessful students. Those who write about the problems of "underachievement" generally focus on modifying the behavior of students to fit a presumably static school system, whereas those who work with the disadvantaged tend to emphasize changing the schools to fit the learning styles of students. Despite the rhetoric that sometimes makes it appear as if one path or the other were the total answer, it is almost certain that some modification is called for in the behaviors of both schools and unsuccessful learners. The present tendency among writers to overemphasize needed changes in the school system seems justified for the simple reason that until now it has been a one-way street, with the student adapting (or failing to adapt) to the demands of the schools. If he did not learn, it was considered his "fault," and he suffered the consequences. There seems no particular merit, however, in attempting to correct this situation by a swing of the pendulum to the equally rigid position of assuming that failure to learn is the sole fault of teachers and schools. At the level of postsecondary education, at least, we will probably make better progress if we regard learning as a joint responsibility of learner and teacher.

A proposal set forth in Chapter 10 posits that a primary goal in the education of New Students is to help them to assume responsibility for their own learning. Indeed, if we do not pass this responsibility to young adults, then we have not done our job in preparing them for a life that will require a never ending capacity to learn new things.

References

ADORNO, T. W., FRENKEL-BRUNSWIK, E., LEVINSON, D. J., AND SANFORD, N. *The Authoritarian Personality.* New York: Harper & Row, 1950.

Behavior Today, May 11, 1970.

BINZEN, P. *Whitetown, USA.* New York: Random House, 1970.

Comparative Guidance and Placement Program (CGP). *Interpretive Manual for Counselors, Administrators, and Faculty, 1969–1970.* New York: College Entrance Examination Board, 1969.

CROSS, K. P. "Is There a Generation Gap?" *The Research Reporter,* 2(3), 1967.

Education, U.S.A., April 27, 1970.

FIELDS, C. M. "Parents of Two Thirds of Today's Students Did Not Go to College, Census Bureau Says." *The Chronicle of Higher Education,* February 15, 1971.

FLANAGAN, J. C., AND ASSOCIATES. *Project TALENT: The American High School Student.* Pittsburgh: Project TALENT, University of Pittsburgh, 1964.

HEIST, P., AND G. YONGE. *Omnibus Personality Inventory Manual, Form F.* New York: The Psychological Corporation, 1968.

KENDRICK, S. A. "The Coming Segregation of Our Selective Colleges." *College Board Review,* 1967–68, *66,* 6–12.

KORNRICH, M. *Underachievement.* Springfield, Ill.: Charles C Thomas, 1965.

RIESSMAN, F. *The Culturally Deprived Child.* New York: Harper & Row, 1962.

SMITH, G. "Usefulness of Peer Ratings of Personality in Educational Research." *Educational and Psychological Measurement,* 1967, *27*(4), 967–984.

THOMAS, C. L., AND J. C. STANLEY. "Effectiveness of High School Grades for Predicting College Grades of Black Students: A Review and Discussion." *Journal of Educational Measurement,* 1969, *6*(4), 203–215.

THORNDIKE, R. L. *The Concepts of Over- and Underachievement.* New York: Teachers College, Columbia University, 1963.

WARREN, J. R. *College Grading Practices: An Overview.* Washington, D.C.: ERIC Clearinghouse on Higher Education, Report 9, March 1971.

INTERESTS OF
NEW STUDENTS

4

An analysis of how people spend their time reveals something about interests; it also tells something about capabilities. The association between interests and abilities is circular and constantly reinforcing. We are likely to engage in those activities that we find interesting; we are likely to find interesting those activities that we do well; and we are likely to do well in those activities that we practice. For example, young people who read well in school tend also to be interested in reading books out of school. Such practice enhances reading ability, which in turn heightens reading interest.

Quite predictably, low-A students tend to spend leisure time in nonacademic pursuits, while high-A students tend to spend more time in activities similar to those taught in school. The indifference of low-ability students to reading is illustrated by data from the ETS Growth Study, which asked a number of questions about how students spend their time. A sample of these items was selected for intensive analysis by ability grouping for this study. High-A students were much more likely to have read almost anything mentioned in the questionnaire than were low-A students. It is well known that high-A students read higher-level materials than low-A students do, but the data also show that high A's simply read more of all types of material—including the comics and sports sections of the newspaper, which can hardly be said to require high levels of reading skills. Of the fifteen questions analyzed that were related to various kinds and levels of reading, only three failed to show large and significant differences in favor of high-A students' greater reading activity outside of school hours. Books telling how to repair, build, or do things and books on hot rods, mechanics, and science fiction showed no differences; low-A boys are as likely to read these books as high-A boys are. As a matter of fact, a fairly substantial number of low-A boys (20 per cent) said that they read such materials regularly. Comic books are read regularly by a small number of students, but low-A students are somewhat more likely to read them than are middle- or high-A youth. Quite the reverse is true, however, when it comes to the comic section of the newspaper; 70 per cent of the high-A students read it regularly, compared with 47 per cent of the low-A students. On all of the more general types of reading, such as *Sports Illustrated, Reader's Digest, Life,* or *Newsweek,* high-A students are roughly twice as likely as low-A students to read the publication regularly. Much of the difference, of course, is accounted for by the greater accessibility of such publications in the homes of students from the higher socioeconomic levels. Research shows clearly the relationship between accessibility of reading material, amount of time spent reading, and level of reading achievement. Research does not answer the age-old question of whether the greater reading activity of high-A students is cause or effect. Does interest in reading lead to high academic achievement, or does academic aptitude lead to greater interest in reading? No doubt, both nature and nurture are involved. The practical problem for educators, however, is that when we are trying to interest eighteen-year-old low-A youth in reading, they have learned to prefer other activities. Our educational task, then, seems to be either to increase the interest of New Students in reading or to use other media through which they will learn. To date, we have concentrated largely on trying to increase their interest—or at least their practice—in reading.

But reading is not the only—and for many people not the primary—way to learn. There are, for example, three major ways of learning about world events: radio or television, newspapers, and news magazines. Growth Study data offer an opportunity to compare practice in the use of various media by low-A and high-A students. For eleventh graders in the study, high-A students were much more likely than low A's to read news magazines regularly (61 per cent to 36 per cent); there was less difference between the groups when it came to reading the newspaper regularly (46 per cent for high A's to 28 per cent for low A's). But there was very little difference in the amount of time spent listening to news on the radio or watching it on television; 36 per cent of the high A's and 29 per cent of the low A's spent more than an hour a week following the news through nonreading media.

Although these data on media leave a number of questions unanswered, such as how much was learned about the news through the various media, the argument is still strong for a much broader use of multimedia in education. The television show *Sesame Street* has been very successful in promoting growth in learning for disadvantaged young children (Ball and Bogatz, 1970); and there are several reasons for suggesting much greater use of new media in the education of older youth: (1) The use of television as a learning tool is novel in the classroom and is not loaded with past experiences of failure for New Students as is the printed page; (2) According to the data presented here, low-A and high-A students get about the same amount of learning practice outside the classroom when television or radio is used to convey information. In reading tasks, low-A students *always* have the handicap. It would be desirable—for both low and high A's—if some learning tasks deliberately tried to avoid a built-in disadvantage for low-A students. (3) Since there may be real individual differences in learning styles, a wide range of teaching tools must be offered if all students are to have equal learning opportunity.

While the *form* in which information is conveyed is an important teaching consideration, there is also evidence that the *content* of the information message has different appeal to high-A and low-A students. Maier and Anderson (1964) used Growth Study data to illustrate orientations of high school students toward the interests associated with adolescent and adult cultures. The adolescent culture was defined by activities that require low levels of cognitive skills and that also stress physical-social content as opposed to intellectual-aesthetic interests. The low-skill dimension, which includes such activities as riding around in cars and watching cartoons on television, has special relevance for many of the characteristics associated with New Students. "The behaviors with low skill requirements," according to Maier and Anderson, "impose few specific demands on the participant, do not provide much feedback to use in guiding action, invite passivity, and provide immediate gratification" (p. 3). Activities of this sort, they hypothesized, would not be conducive to cognitive growth. The words of their description have a familiar ring. Data presented in Chapter 3 showed the passive learning stance and the desire for immediate gratification evidenced by New Students in their response to personality questionnaires. According to Maier and Anderson, these attitudes would be expected from young people participating largely in the adolescent culture.

Maier and Anderson and other theorists subscribing to an interactionist view of cognitive development reject the notion of the fixed or innate I.Q., maintaining that cognitive abilities are developed when readiness to learn and appropriate learning experiences are brought together (see Hunt, 1969; Piaget, 1947). The lack of cognitive experiences in the environments of low-A youngsters, they maintain, impedes intellectual development. Therefore, adolescents who spend large amounts of time in activities that require low cognitive effort will lag behind classmates with greater cognitive experience.

There is considerable research support for the interactionist view of cognitive development, since low-A youth do tend to spend their spare time in activities with low potential for intellectual development, whereas high-A youth gravitate toward intellectually stimulating activities out of school as well as in school. The greatest differences between the interests of low-A and high-A youth in the Growth Study sample are on a cognitive/noncognitive dimension. Almost twice as many low-A youth as high-A students (45 to 24 per cent) spend over an hour a week watching teen-age music and dancing programs. Low-A youth are also much more likely to date once a week or more often (32 per cent for low A's to 17 per cent for high A's). As predicted by the interaction hypothesis, high-A students spend considerably more time than low-A youth in cognitive activities. Twice as many high A's as low A's spend two hours a week or more practicing, arranging, or composing music (27 per cent to 13 per cent) and have read more than two books during the year about history, current events, or biography (32 per cent to 16 per cent).

Some activities that might be hypothesized to have low potential for cognitive development did not differentiate at all between low-A and high-A youth. "Hanging around, just loafing, talking, or snacking with friends" seems to be a universal teen-age activity, with 41 per cent of the high A's and 41 per cent of the low A's spending more than two hours a week at it. All types of athletic activities—from attending athletic events once a week or more often (44 per cent for both high and low A's) to spending two hours a week or more practicing sports (30 per cent for both groups)—appear common to all young people, regardless of academic ability.

In summary, some noncognitive activities are part of the adolescent subculture in which all teen-agers have an interest. But data showing the predominant interest of low-A youth in noncognitive activities are abundant. Generally speaking, when high school seniors and college freshmen are asked about their preferences for various out-of-school activities, students who score high on measures of academic achievement are prone to show high interest in intellectually challenging activities and occupations. Students who score low on academic aptitude and achievement measures are more likely to indicate interest in activities calling largely for noncognitive skills.

The effect of poor academic-skill development on 18-year-old youth is apparent in students' perceptions of themselves and their development. The research shows clear differences by ability groupings in the things that students say they do well. High school seniors in the SCOPE study were offered a list of nine activities and asked to indicate the *one* which they felt they did best. The largest percentage of high-A girls chose "read" (26 per cent); for high-A boys the first choice was "work with numbers and mathematics" (27 per cent). The ability to read well was not a likely choice for low-A girls (17 per cent) or even for high-A boys (14 per cent). Self-assessment of reading ability is subject to wide variation, with girls showing more confidence than boys and high A's more confidence than low A's. The research argues strongly for decreasing the heavy emphasis on reading in school learning situations and using alternative methods that have a greater potential for securing the interest of lower-A youth and of young males in general.

The clear activity preference for low-A girls in the SCOPE sample was "sewing and cooking" (28 per cent), while low-A boys chose "working with tools" (28 per cent) and "sports" (27 per cent). The middle A's fell, as usual, in between: 21 per cent of the girls chose cooking and sewing, followed closely by the 20 per cent who selected reading; middle-A boys chose sports (29 per cent) followed by working with tools (22 per cent).

At the college level, the story is the same. The questionnaire used in the annual survey of college freshmen conducted by the American Council on Education (Panos, Astin, and Creager, 1967) asked students to indicate which of thirty activities they could do well. The differences between students at two-year colleges and at universities are roughly comparable to the distinction we have been making between New Students and traditional students, since only 37 per cent of the two-year students but 69 per cent of the university students had high school grade averages of *B* or better. A larger proportion of university students than two-year-college students said they could perform twenty-five of the thirty activities well, indicating the greater self-confidence of high-ability students. But on some nonacademic activities greater proportions of students at two-year colleges rated their achievement high. Two-year-college women, for example, were more likely than university-freshman women to say that they could do the following things well: type forty words per minute, use a sewing machine, mix a martini, set a table for a formal party, bake a cake from scratch, and do at least fifteen pushups. For men, the pattern is similar but not as clear because of the nature of the activities on the list.

Project TALENT obtained the same pattern of nonacademic interests on the part of low-A youth by asking about hobbies. More than three times as many low-A males as high-A males (28 per cent to 8 per cent) stated that they often engage in woodworking or metalworking activities; and 44 per cent of the low A's, compared with 28 per cent of the high A's, profess to a hobby of repairing cars. Although the figures are not quite so dramatic for girls, there are also significant differences in preferences for the hobbies of cooking and sewing, with roughly a 10 per cent difference in favor of the low-A girls.

No matter what kind of measurement is used—sophisticated interest scales, leisure-time activities, hobby preference, ability self-evaluations—the outcome is much the same: New Students generally express their greatest interest in activities that are not ordinarily stressed in the schools. If New Students seek recognition for skills in which they consider themselves most competent, they are likely to have to go outside the formal school system to find it. While high A's are using their strongest abilities in school, low A's must demonstrate one of their weaker abilities. No wonder the academic-performance gap widens as students proceed through school (Coleman, 1966).

The primarily nonacademic interests of New Students can be explained negatively as a flight *from* academic activities—or they can be viewed positively as an attraction *to* other kinds of interests. For example, a girl who consistently gets *D* in reading in school is not likely to say that reading is a special interest. On the other hand, she may have developed a *positive* interest in sewing and, as a result, developed high-level skills such as working with color, form, and texture; dealing with problems of spatial perception and pattern matching; following complex instructions and diagrams—to say nothing of developing a high degree of skill in eye-hand coordination.

Data from the new Comparative Guidance and Placement Program (CGP) of the College Board show strong *positive interest profiles* for New Students. The first year of experience with these tests revealed that students enrolled in the various curricula had distinctive profiles of interests that transcended the type of institution they were attending.

In order to gain a further understanding of the positive interests and motivations of some groups of New Students, I selected for special attention three groups of New Students, representing distinctive interest profiles on the Comparative Interest Index of the CGP. The selection of particular interest groups was based upon the size of the sample available. There were three interest patterns exhibited by 200 or more students. Subgroup A consisted of 225 women who scored in the lowest third on the criterion test of academic ability but who made above-average scores on two tests measuring interests in business and in secretarial tasks. Subgroup B consisted of 256 low-A women with above-average scores on the two scales measuring interest in health and biology. Subgroup C consisted of 212 low-A women who scored high on interest in social sciences (the only common element in the rather nondistinctive profile of an independent sample of 1967 freshmen who enrolled in college-parallel liberal-arts curricula).

In looking carefully at these interest data, we are focusing on the strengths of low-A women, not upon their weaknesses. The three groups share low-A status; they all meet the criterion for classification as New Students to higher education. But they are women who scored *above* the average of all two-year-college women in certain curricular-related interests. Table 13 shows the percentage of each group giving various responses to selected items of the Biographical Inventory of the CGP.

Immediately apparent is the consistency with which strong interest profiles separate low-A two-year college women with different educational and career interests. The subgroups are formed on the basis of interest tests alone, not on curricular enrollments; but even as undifferentiated as the liberal-arts interest profile is, 92 per cent of the low-A women with very high interests in the social sciences are enrolled in college-parallel liberal-arts curricula. The Social Science Scale calls for a self-rating of interest on items such as "To take part in discussions of current events both in school and at home," "To study and discuss what our government should do about foreign affairs," and "To find out when certain historic events took place, when certain famous people lived, etc." Table 13 indicates that low-A women who like to do such things also tend to prefer an academic life, are enrolled in a college-parallel liberal-arts curriculum, liked English and social studies in high school, and are not inclined to view their education as primarily vocational. The item on ethnic identity indicates that low-A black women are somewhat less likely than Caucasians to express interests consistent with the liberal-arts pattern. The relatively large percentages of blacks in all three interest subgroups, compared with the percentage in the population of community college women (19 per cent), reflects the large number of minority students scoring in the lowest third on the traditional measure of academic aptitude. Not shown is Table 13 but derived from original data is the ethnic distribution of the low-A

Table 13. RESPONSES TO BIOGRAPHICAL INVENTORY
ITEMS BY LOW-A WOMEN IN THREE INTEREST SUBGROUPS

	Interest Subgroups			All Women in CGP Sample
	Business	Health	Liberal Arts	
	Per Cent			
Kind of life preferred				
Academic (teaching, research, etc.)	8	13	68	26
Business (management, marketing, etc.)	62	2	3	12
Professional (doctor, lawyer, etc.)	1	50	4	11
Home and family	12	11	11	19
Undecided	8	8	6	14
Other	8	17	8	17
Junior College Curriculum				
College-parallel	15	9	92	51
Career 2-year	52	58	6	32
Career 1½-year	32	31	0	2
Other	1	2	2	10
Subject most liked in high school				
English	24	18	28	27
Mathematics	10	11	5	9
Physical education	13	8	10	12
Sciences	4	35	5	11
Shop or commercial	26	2	2	6
Social sciences	11	13	29	14
Other	11	13	21	21

Table 13. (Cont.) Responses to Biographical Inventory
Items by Low-A Women in Three Interest Subgroups

| | Interest Subgroups | | | All Women in CGP Sample |
	Business	Health	Liberal Arts	
Time spent thinking about future career				
Much more than others	15	28	15	11
Somewhat more	70	60	67	66
Somewhat or much less	16	12	18	23
Would like counseling on educational and vocational plans and opportunities	73	75	79	69
Know exactly work desired after education	31	65	38	28
Purpose of education— mostly or entirely job training	60	54	24	42
Ethnic Identity				
Caucasian	35	34	55	74
Black American	54	56	38	19
Other	11	9	7	7

Source: CGP data, 1969.

female group, which is 43 per cent Caucasian, 44 per cent black, and 13 per cent other.

New Students scoring high on CGP interest tests appear quite positively attracted to their field of study. Low-A women interested in activities associated with health (for instance, liking to maintain charts of temperatures and blood pressure, or to make a sick person comfortable) and with biology (liking to experiment with plants or to test soil conditions) present an especially strong picture of career motivation. Despite a rather poor academic background, they are more likely than the average community college woman to have enjoyed science courses in high school—and to have rejected the more common female interest in English. They are much more likely than the average community college woman to know exactly what line of work they want to enter and to spend time thinking about their future careers.

Women with strong interests in business and secretarial activities on the Comparative Interest Index are likely to view education as job preparation, but they are not as sharply focused toward a specific career as are the women interested in the health fields. Compared with women in general, however, business-oriented women, like their health-oriented classmates, present a picture of positive interests. We would expect them to do well in school work that capitalizes on these interests.

The Student Satisfaction Questionnaire of the CGP shows how well satisfied some of these New Students are with their field of study in the community college. The Satisfaction Questionnaire asks community college students to indicate their reactions to their educations. Some 27,000 students responded to the Questionnaire in the fall of 1968. The tabulation of these responses (CGP, 1968) included both males and females, but the percentage of responses to selected items are presented in Table 14 for the same fields of study as those of Table 13.

As a group, students enrolled in the health curricula (mostly women) stand out for their exuberant satisfaction with their choice. In general, students in the health curricula are more certain of their direction and better satisfied with their training than any other curricular group. Business students in the nondegree curricula are more highly motivated and better satisfied than those in the two-year degree programs. The data confirm the notion that students in the college-parallel liberal-arts curricula generally are preparing for further schooling rather than for a vocation; and it is also clear that many liberal-arts students have not yet decided what vocation they wish to pursue. Whether this indecision is cause or effect is an open question. Do people who are uncertain of career interests enroll in liberal-arts courses, or do liberal-arts students delay career decisions because they look forward to more years of school-

Table 14. RESPONSES TO STUDENT SATISFACTION QUESTIONNAIRE
BY THREE CURRICULAR SUBGROUPS (MALE AND FEMALE)

	Business	Health	Liberal Arts	All Students
	Per Cent			
Plan to stay in program	47–56*	67–74*	39	43
Program will prepare me for job I want	46–61	67	34	40
Looking forward to later courses in the field	39–45	60–31	48	45
Courses in program relate to future plan	39–57	58	27	34
Have definitely decided what to major in	43	69–51	31	38
Don't need better training than getting	23–43	44–53	11	16
Have definite plans for vocation	29–35	59–50	30	30
Chosen vocation will afford good income	42–51	55–29	33	35
Have not changed mind several times about vocation	35–40	63	33	36
Read about vocation outside courses	12	26	16	15
Will like job	39–52	67	26	33
Courses are right level of difficulty	29–35	40	29	28
Taking courses wanted to take	34–51	45–66	33	33
Find texts hard to read	24–44	30–54	24	24

Source: CGP, Phase II, 1968.

* Where percentages differ significantly, the first listed refers to students enrolled in two-year programs and the second to those in one-year to year-and-a-half programs.

ing? Perhaps both influences operate to give liberal-arts students vaguer goals.

From these specific observations, we can posit a general prediction that students who have sharply focused career interests are likely to be better satisfied with their career training than students who are less certain about their vocational interests. For example, when students were asked to respond to the item "I need better training than I get in my program," the percentages disagreeing— indicating that their training was adequate—appeared in the following order: vocational health fields (nondegree), 53 per cent; technical health fields (degree), 44 per cent; vocational business fields (nondegree), 43 per cent; degree business programs, 23 per cent; and liberal-arts transfer programs, 11 per cent.

These data on vocational interests, then, reveal rather clear patterns of interests and positive motivations and satisfactions of young people in vocational curricula. There is nothing in the data on health interest subgroups, for example, to suggest that these are students who could not succeed in traditional academic courses and therefore took vocational courses as second best. To the contrary, the data show clear positive attractions to the health curricula.

Interests, like other student characteristics, differentiate New Students from traditional students not so much in amount as in kind. The prestige bias against the interests of New Students is illustrated by the fact that we must use a negative word—nonacademic—to describe those interests. There is clear evidence that New Students are not as interested in academic pursuits as are traditional students. This lack of interest, accompanied as it is by lack of practice and familiarity with academic subject matter, is most assuredly a handicap to New Students in school. According to interactionist theorists, the adherence of New Students to the adolescent culture is an obstacle to maximum cognitive development.

It would be difficult and undesirable to argue that schools do not have a responsibility to expose New Students to academic subjects in ways that stimulate interest. On the other hand, education can be faulted for not capitalizing on the strong positive interests shown by New Students. Nonacademic interests are not necessarily noncognitive, nor are opportunities for learning limited to conventional classroom materials. There are cognitive and creative challenges to be found in constructing things from metal, wood, and fabrics. Traditional students as well as New Students could benefit from the stimulation and cultivation of abilities such as spatial perception, eye-hand coordination, and the reading and following of directions. Likewise, use of a variety of ways of conveying information—television, audio-visual aids, drama—would be advantageous to all students. The traditional academic curriculum has catered to the strengths of traditional students and has forced New Students to develop their special strengths out of the classroom. Variety in method and in content is long overdue in education at all levels.

Unfortunately, the intellectual community has frequently been guilty of pressuring for its own system of values and interests. As long as a unidimensional value system is perpetuated, comparisons will be made in terms of higher and lower, better and poorer, above average and below average. In other words, there will always be a "lowest third" in any system that demands conformity to a single brand of excellence—even if the brand name is intellectualism.

References

BALL, S., AND G. A. BOGATZ. *The First Year of* Sesame Street: *An Evaluation.* Princeton: Educational Testing Service, PR-70-15, 1970.

COLEMAN, J., ET AL. *Equality of Educational Opportunities.* Washington, D.C.: Government Printing Office, 1966.

Comparative Guidance and Placement Program (CGP). *Cross-College Distribution of Responses to Student Questionnaire.* Prepared for the College Entrance Examination Board. Princeton: Educational Testing Service, 1968.

————. *Interpretative Manual for Counselors, Administrators, and Faculty, 1969–70.* New York: College Entrance Examination Board, 1969.

HUNT, J. MC V. "Has Compensatory Education Failed? Has It Been Attempted?" *Harvard Educational Review,* 1969, *39*(2), 278–300.

MAIER, M., AND S. ANDERSON. *Growth Study: Adolescent Behavior and Interests.* Research Bulletin RB-64-52. Princeton: Educational Testing Service, October 1964.

PANOS, R. J., A. W. ASTIN, AND J. A. CREAGER. *National Norms for Entering College Freshmen—Fall 1967*. Washington, D.C.: American Council on Education, 1967.

PIAGET, J. *The Psychology of Intelligence*. London: Routledge and Kegan Paul, 1947.

NEW STUDENTS LOOK
AT EDUCATION

5

Going to school is the most important activity in a young person's life. The experiences and the credentials of education are vitally important—to the formation of self-concept, to status, and to vocational and personal futures. Considerable attention was devoted in Chapter 2 to some of the effects of the invisible curriculum on the self-concepts of children who rank in the bottom third of the class. In this chapter, we shall first examine some of the reactions of New Students to their past school experiences. Second, we shall look at the expectations held by New Students for their future education. What do they want from college? What kind of college would they like to attend? What type of curricular program do they seek? And how might colleges be of more assistance to them? Finally, we shall present some data regarding student reactions to their first year of college. How has the college experience changed them and to what do they attribute the changes?

Reactions to Past Education

Generally speaking, schools have done a better job of educating youth for continuing in the school system than they have of preparing them to lead useful and productive lives. As they evaluate their educational experiences, students seem to recognize the centrality given to academic preparation for further schooling. Students in the SCOPE sample were most likely to rate their high school courses as "very useful" in preparing them for college; 54 per cent did so. They were less likely to rate high school courses as useful for job preparation (38 per cent) or as preparation for the assumption of adult responsibilities (38 per cent). This emphasis means that high-A students, 80 per cent of whom were headed for college, generally considered their high school training relevant to their immediate futures; three fourths of them rated high school courses very useful for college preparation. Only 47 per cent of the low-A students felt equally enthusiastic about high school courses as preparation for a job. Junior college students express the same kinds of feelings. Those who later transferred to four-year colleges were more likely to rate their junior college experiences as helpful or extremely helpful (97 per cent) than were those who went directly to work (79 per cent) (Florida Community Junior College Interinstitutional Research Council, 1969).

Although New Students are not as likely as traditional students to perceive the schools as directly relevant to their interests, they seem to harbor no resentment against the most visible representatives of the system—the teachers. Low-A students are almost as likely as high-A students to feel that their teachers usually understand them (59 per cent for low A's to 63 per cent for high A's) and that their teachers treat them fairly (85 per cent to 93 per cent). And almost three quarters of the students—low A, middle A, or high A—feel that the things they "have to study in school are important."

The *differences* between the attitudes of New Students and traditional students toward high school appear in their responses to items that are related to the system itself or perhaps to the emphasis on academic competition. For example, low-A students are much more likely than high-A students to say that they would do better work in school if their teachers did not go so fast (28 per cent to 9 per cent). They are also more likely to feel "nervous, tense, or shy" in class (38 per cent to 21 per cent).

When high school seniors participating in the SCOPE survey were asked what changes they would make if they were running

the school, it was clear that most students would make changes; only 12 per cent would "keep school just as it is." Low-A students, however, would move in the direction of adding more practical courses to help students get jobs (71 per cent to 53 per cent for the high-A group), whereas high-A students advocate improvements such as adding more books to the library (74 per cent to 58 per cent for low-A students). There were no major differences between aptitude groups on such generally "good" ideas as providing more time to talk with counselors about school and vocations (69 per cent), having more class discussions instead of lectures (66 per cent), or allowing students greater freedom in choosing courses (50 per cent).

The support for individualization of educational programs is strong in these data. While New Students and traditional students may want different things from the schools, both groups want more attention to their particular needs and the opportunity to make choices.

Expectations of College

Since low-A as well as high-A students are now beginning to contemplate college attendance and to make college choices, what can be said about their expectations of what college should offer?

Students in general would like college to be a pleasant experience where people are friendly and helpful. When high school seniors were asked to select descriptions of the college they would like to attend, the largest proportion (53 per cent) of all students regardless of ability expressed a preference for the college description that read,

At this college there are many activities, and students are encouraged to take part. The professors go out of their way to make sure that students understand the classwork, and everyone is friendly on the campus.

For low-A students a very close runner-up in the preferred college was vocationally oriented:

At this college students are preparing for a particular job or career. They are mostly interested in courses which train them for

occupations they have chosen. Many of the students are working part-time to pay for their education.

Thirty-seven per cent of the low-A students picked this college as the one they would most like to attend. It was selected by only 15 per cent of the high-A students, who were more likely (21 per cent) to prefer the traditional academic model:

At this college there are many good students who try to get top grades. Professors expect them to study a lot, but frequently are willing to discuss such things as current world affairs and other serious topics outside of classes. The students enjoy going to concerts and lectures given on campus.

If we could combine the friendly atmosphere conveyed in the first model with the academic emphasis of the third college described, hypothetically we would satisfy 82 per cent of the high-A students: 61 per cent preferred the friendly model; 21 per cent, the academic model. Likewise, if we combined the friendly model with a vocational emphasis, we could satisfy 82 per cent of the low-A students: 45 per cent of them chose the friendly model, and 37 per cent opted for the vocational model. Students scoring in the middle third of the class had preferences similar to those of the low-A group: 57 per cent preferred the friendly college; 29 per cent preferred the vocational model; only 8 per cent chose the description of the academically oriented college.

Although the academic model is the one that many educators admire, it is not popular among high school seniors; only 13 per cent of the total group, without regard to ability, gave it first preference when asked which college they would wish to attend. Dunham (1969) has described in some detail faculty pressures to push state colleges toward greater academic and research emphases —toward emulating prestige colleges and universities. There is also considerable evidence that many community college faculty members tend to pattern their professional aspirations along the traditional lines of the academic model (Cross, 1971a). Since almost all college faculty—junior college, senior college, or university—came from the group of students that are here labeled traditional, it is not surprising that their interests and those of today's traditional college students should coincide along intellectual dimensions. But that is all the more reason for concern: Patterning egalitarian colleges after the kind of education that appeals to faculty can be a step backward for New Students. There is a New Student to higher education. His needs and interests are different from those of traditional college students, and, perhaps even more important, they are different from those of traditional faculty members.

The fourth college description offered in the SCOPE Questionnaire has little appeal to New Students or to traditional students. Fundamentally it can be considered anti-intellectual and anti-purposeful:

At this college most students go to athletic events. Most students do not study on Saturdays and feel free to go to movies during the week. Everyone has a lot of fun. Many of the girls at this school expect to be married as soon as they graduate.

Only 6 per cent of the students endorsed "fun college" as their first choice. But low-A students were more likely to choose it than high-A students (9 per cent, 6 per cent, and 3 per cent for the three aptitude groups), and boys were twice as likely to choose it as girls.

What, more specifically, are the elements of the campus environment that influence college choice? Unlike the data discussed in the paragraphs above, the percentages shown in Table 15 are based upon students who plan to go to college or are not yet sure; those who plan no type of postsecondary education are excluded.

While a large majority (84 per cent) of the high-A students stress that the reputation of the faculty for good teaching is a major consideration in choosing a college, a healthy majority (66 per cent) of the low-A group also feel that good teaching is a requisite for a good college. The emphasis on a pleasant atmosphere peopled with good teachers predominates for all three aptitude groups. The appeal of an intellectual atmosphere is quite strong for the high-A students but has less appeal than any other characteristic offered for low-A students. The financial aspects of college choice do not appear to differentiate between aptitude groups as much as might be expected. If low cost, offers of financial aid, and nearness to home are considered together, however, low-A students give con-

Table 15. HIGH SCHOOL SENIORS RATING SELECTED COLLEGE
CHARACTERISTICS A "MAJOR CONSIDERATION" IN CHOICE

	Low A	Middle A	High A
	Per Cent		
Reputation of faculty for good teaching	66	77	84
Friendly social climate	56	63	59
Low cost	43	45	39
Offer of scholarship or other financial aid	38	32	31
Close to home	34	34	28
Intellectual atmosphere	28	29	40

Source: SCOPE data, 1966.

siderably more weight than high-A students to these factors of cost. This is to be expected, since low-A students are predominantly students from low socioeconomic backgrounds.

Not included in this particular set of item alternatives is one choice that is considered major to many people selecting a college— the choice of the course of study. Reference to data collected from students entering two-year colleges in the fall of 1970 (CGP, 1971) helps to shed some light on that question. Students registering for the transfer curricula in two-year colleges were most likely to say that they chose the two-year institution because it was close to home (26 per cent) and because of its low cost (16 per cent). Thus, the data for two-year colleges present the unusual situation in which the better students are attracted to the college more for its convenience than for its educational program; less able students are attracted by the educational strength of the institution. The apparent explanation is that traditional students can be served by almost any college offering the traditional course of study, whereas community colleges have a special educational mission in providing career programs for New Students.

If we were to draw a profile of an attractive college for a typical New Student based upon a composite of the preferences revealed in questionnaire data, the college might be pictured something like this: It is a friendly place where good teaching is emphasized and where faculty members take an interest in students. It offers courses clearly relevant to career preparation, stressing the development of skills over the manipulation of abstract concepts. Low cost, while presumably an advantage to all New Students, might offer the only educational opportunity for low-income students who are interested in traditional academic subjects. As a matter of fact, the institution favored by New Students is beginning to look very much like some of today's better comprehensive community colleges.

Requests for Assistance

Just as students entering colleges have differing preferences, motives, and expectations, they also have varying needs. Some of these needs are expressed by the answers of entering community college freshmen to some questions in the CGP battery. The Biographical Inventory contains an Assistance Guide, wherein students may indicate the areas in which special help is desired from the college. Although there has been some feeling among counselors that New Students are resistant to counseling, the data show that New Students generally are eager for all types of assistance. At least they express the need for help on a written questionnaire. (See Table 16.)

The greatest differences between low-A and high-A students fall just where expected—in those areas most obviously related to conventional school success. Since the low-A category throughout this study is defined by scores in the lowest third on a verbal test, it is to be expected that these students would feel inadequate in reading skills. As a matter of fact, however, a very large number of community college students at all levels of aptitude express a need for help in developing the requisite skills for college work. The community colleges have read this plea correctly. In response to my spring 1970 questionnaire inquiring what provisions community colleges were making for New Students, 92 per cent of the responders replied that they offered remedial or developmental courses to upgrade verbal or other academic skills; 76 per cent offered financial aids especially designed for disadvantaged students;

Table 16. ENTERING JUNIOR COLLEGE STUDENTS
DESIRING ASSISTANCE WITH VARIOUS PROBLEMS

	Low A	Middle A	High A	Total
	Per Cent			
Counseling about educational and vocational plans	63	65	65	64
Help in developing good study techniques	76	69	58	69
Help to increase reading speed and comprehension	67	56	46	57
Help finding full- or part-time employment	44	37	38	39
Financial aid	35	30	32	32
Counseling about personal problems	26	18	16	20

Source: CGP data, 1969.

and 61 per cent provided special counseling. (See Appendix C for complete questionnaire responses.) A substantial proportion of New Students express a desire for help in all three of these areas.

Although the access programs of the 1960s concentrated more on the provision of financial assistance to students than they did on educational programming, the community college students represented in the figures in Table 16 rate financial assistance less important than educational assistance. High school students, too, are more concerned with the educational barriers to college than they are with the financial barriers. When SCOPE seniors were asked to state the one most likely reason they might fail to enter college, one third of the low-A students replied, "My grades are not good enough"; only 12 per cent regarded lack of money as the major barrier to college attendance. When college freshmen in the SCOPE study were asked to indicate likely reasons why they might drop out of school, financial reasons ranked below military service (46 per cent for men), academic problems (34 per cent), lack of interest

(24 per cent), and marriage (27 per cent for women). The cost of tuition and fees (18 per cent) was perceived as a little more threatening to continued schooling than the loss of outside financial help (14 per cent).

There are, however, some important sex differences appearing in the student financial-need data. The largest reservoir of academically able students not now continuing their education beyond high school consists of women who are above average in ability and below average in socioeconomic status (see Chapter 1). Many of these women are just beginning to enter public community colleges, and their need for financial assistance is much greater than their need for special educational programs. Among the six problem areas listed in Table 16 there were no important sex differences in the percentages of students desiring college assistance *except* on the need for help on study techniques (60 per cent of the men and 55 per cent of the women) and on the two items related to financing education. Women were more likely than men to need help finding a job (41 per cent to 32 per cent) and to request financial aid (32 per cent to 26 per cent) (CGP, 1971).

The sex differences in requests for financial aid were especially large among the New Student group. Forty-three per cent of the low-A women and 32 per cent of the low-A men indicated a desire for financial aid, while 54 per cent of the low-A women and 40 per cent of the low-A men requested help finding full- or part-time jobs. There is little doubt that college women have a more difficult time finding jobs than do men. Also, women may be somewhat more prone to enter junior college without jobs, whereas men are more reluctant to be dependent upon parental assistance if financial aid is not forthcoming. As postsecondary education becomes more essential and women receive greater encouragement to attend college, the number of women needing financial assistance is likely to climb accordingly. It is not likely that job opportunities for women will expand as rapidly as educational opportunities. Hence, lower pay and fewer job opportunities for women may throw a disproportionate female need on the financial resources of colleges.

Although Table 16 shows that counseling help for personal problems is desired less often than any of the six services listed in the Assistance Guide, New Students are more likely to indicate a desire for personal counseling than are traditional students. A great deal has been written about the home problems of low-SES youth, and we have devoted considerable attention to the stressful environments of the schools for low-A youth. There are no very comprehensive studies of the specific nature of the personal problems of New Students as compared with those of traditional students, however. We have commented upon the fact that low-A students are more likely to feel tense in class than high-A students, and a second item on the SCOPE questionnaire provides some clue about the nature of some problems at home faced by New Students. Among the college freshmen who answered the SCOPE questionnaire, 18 per cent of the low-A males and 12 per cent of the low-A females (compared to 10 per cent of the high-A males and females) admitted to problems with the generation gap by indicating that being in conflict with parents was descriptive of them in their first year at college. Since one of the characteristics of New Students is that in attending college they are doing something quite foreign to anything their parents have done, the existence of a generation gap is not surprising. It may be more appropriately perceived as an educational gap than an age gap, however.

The relationship between personal problems and low academic achievement can be regarded as cause or effect or both. Young people with personal problems are unable to devote full attention to school work. In this sense, the personal problems are the cause of poor school achievement. On the other hand, according to the theory advanced in Chapter 2, the failure of low-A students to do well in the competition of the classroom may create personal feelings of doubt and insecurity. Whichever came first—the poor school performance or the personal problems—once the cycle starts, it tends to reinforce itself. Personal problems can lead to poor school performance, which in turn may lead to problems of self-doubt and self-dissatisfaction, which, added to the further burden of poor grades, may increase personal insecurity. While the schools cannot be expected to solve the personal and home problems of students, they can offer personal counseling for a period in life that many young people find quite difficult. Most important, schools can begin to make some of the fundamental changes that would remove the fear-of-failure and personal-threat syndrome from the educational experience. There is reason to suspect that the forced competition of young people along narrow academic dimensions is responsible for creating some special problems for New Students and for exacerbating others.

Influence of College

When college students in the SCOPE sample were asked to evaluate their progress during their first year of college, most students (63 per cent of the New Students and 56 per cent of the traditional students) felt that they had made considerable progress in improving their ability to get along with different kinds of people. In fact, more students felt that they had made progress in interpersonal relations than in any of the five other objectives listed. New Students ranked the development of career skills second (45 per cent for low A's to 24 per cent for high A's), whereas traditional students were somewhat more likely to indicate progress in developing intellectual interests (48 per cent for high A's to 41 per cent for low A's).

It is interesting to observe that the skill most likely to be developed in the first year of college is one that is frequently considered incidental to the educational enterprise. Furthermore, low-A students, most of whom are enrolled in commuter colleges, are somewhat *more* likely to feel that they have made progress in learning how to get along with people than are high-A students, most of whom are enrolled in residential colleges, where dormitories, fraternities, and a greater number of on-campus social activities provide experience in relating to other people.

The relative influence of different kinds of people in the college environment on low-A and high-A students is a matter of some interest. New Students were most likely to attribute changes in attitudes on social issues to the influence of outside speakers or activists (18 per cent); fellow students were the next most likely source of influence (11 per cent), followed by teachers (7 per cent) and student leaders (6 per cent). For high A's the order was fellow students (19 per cent), outside speakers or activists (11 per cent), teachers (7 per cent), and student leaders (3 per cent). Apparently neither of the formal, recognized channels of influence—teachers

or student leaders—has much effect on student attitudes regarding
social issues. The relatively great effect of "outside speakers or activists" on low-A students is difficult to interpret because of the conjunction of two rather different sources of influence. If we assume
that outside speakers and activists both play the role of "expert" on
a specific topic to a voluntary gathering of students, then the explanation of the findings may lie in the greater willingness of low-A
students to accept the word of authorities, which is a major characteristic of the authoritarian personality discussed in Chapter 3. There
is also the fact that at the time these data were collected, in 1967,
students on four-year-college campuses were more actively engaged
in discussing Vietnam, protest movements, and civil rights issues
than were students on two-year campuses. Recently, however, community college students have taken a more active role in discussing
these issues of national concern, and were we to collect data today,
we might find that community college students were attributing
increasing amounts of attitude influence to fellow students.

If educators cannot take much credit for student progress
in interpersonal relationships, they may perhaps take some credit
for the areas that students ranked second. As mentioned, a large
number of New Students (45 per cent) felt that they had made a
great deal of progress in developing skills and techniques directly
applicable to a job, but few high-A students (24 per cent) felt that
career development had been an outcome of their first year in college. High-A students (48 per cent) were more likely to feel that
they had developed intellectual interests and a greater appreciation
of ideas. The differences are to be expected if the vocational curricula, in which many New Students are enrolled, and the academic
curricula, which traditional students tend to pursue, are doing their
jobs. According to the students, they are.

Only about one fourth of the students admitted much
progress in developing critical-thinking skills and an increased appreciation of the arts; and low A's were as likely as high A's to feel
that progress had been made in these areas. An interesting difference
between New Students and traditional students appeared in the
percentages saying that they had made good progress in developing
a satisfying philosophy of life. For New Students, it ranked fairly
high, with 32 per cent claiming progress; for traditional students,

it ranked the lowest of six areas listed (24 per cent). Perhaps the imminent approach of adult responsibilities for two-year-college students creates a more urgent need to develop a philosophy of life.

The overall reaction of students to their first year of college is heartening. Few students felt that little or no progress had been made, but there were differences between low A's and high A's in two areas of development. High A's were more likely than low A's to feel that they had made no progress toward the development of skills applicable to a job (26 per cent to 11 per cent) and that no progress had been made in developing a satisfying philosophy of life (24 per cent to 13 per cent). Perhaps the high-A students feel they have plenty of time—56 per cent of them say they expect to get at least a master's degree. Exactly the same percentage of low-A students expect to be faced immediately with the practical problems of life—56 per cent of them expect to leave school with less than a bachelor's degree.

An analysis of students' perceptions of their educational experiences leads to some broad conclusions and speculations. First, there is evidence that New Students are more uncomfortable in the traditional academic educational system than are the students for whom present educational experiences were designed. They are more likely than traditional students to feel that the academic pace is too fast for them; they are more likely to feel nervous or shy in the competitive classroom; they are more eager for college assistance with problems related to academic achievement, and they are more interested in counseling help with personal problems.

Second, there is evidence that New Students have some ideas about what they would like schools and colleges to do. They are likely to be attracted to courses and colleges that are seen as practical preparation for their vocational futures. The data support a broad generalization that New Students are eager to take on their adult responsibilities. New Students attending community colleges indicate feelings of progress in learning how to get along with people, in learning job-related skills, and in developing a satisfactory philosophy of life.

Third, New Students to higher education face some of the same problems faced by all pioneers into new ventures. Their lives become a mixture of the old and out of date and the new and not quite ready. Their parents and homes may present a way of life that is no longer adequate for them—and yet the new life promised by higher education is not quite ready for them. Traditional students and traditional faculty members perpetuate their own scheme of values. Although New Students show some satisfactions with traditional vocational education, it is not sufficient to separate higher education into two tracks—academic and vocational.

Narrow vocational education can be just as narrow as traditional academic education and probably considerably more damaging to the occupational futures of students. It is possible now that a narrowly trained vocational student will be outdated by the time he graduates; and with the rapid technological changes steadily taking place in industry, new job skills almost certainly will be needed several times during the lifetime of the average worker. In all probability, he will need retraining and the community colleges will need great flexibility and imagination to meet these needs. Skill training in vocational education may be but a small part of the future task. The self-confidence and flexibility to try new things and a generalized approach to problem-solving will almost certainly be requirements for both professional and skilled workers of the future. It is probably fair to say that neither traditional academic education nor traditional vocational education has given much attention to the personal development of the individual who is required to cope with modern society. It is not very likely that teachers can continue to teach academic and vocational skills in the classroom and hope that somehow the counseling staff will attend to "personal development."

There is no question that the ability to solve problems—whether they be problems of human distress tackled by a social worker, problems of stalled machinery approached by a skilled mechanic, or methods of smog control studied by a Ph.D. scientist—is an equally appropriate goal for vocational or academic education. The function of education should be to provide alternate pathways to personal development and self-fulfillment.

References

Comparative Guidance and Placement Program. *Program Summary Statistics—1970–71*. Prepared for the College Entrance Examination Board. Princeton: Educational Testing Service, 1971.

CROSS, K. P. "The Role of the Junior College in Providing Postsecondary Education for All." *Trends in Postsecondary Education*. Washington, D.C.: Office of Education, Government Printing Office, 1971. a

——————. "Access and Accommodation in Higher Education." The White House Conference on Youth. Berkeley: Center for Research and Development in Higher Education, University of California, 1971. b

DUNHAM, E. A. *Colleges of the Forgotten Americans*. New York: McGraw-Hill, 1969.

Florida Community Junior College Inter-Institutional Research Council. *Where Are They Now?* A Follow-Up Study of First-Time College Freshmen in Florida's Community Colleges in Fall 1966. Gainesville: Institute of Higher Education, University of Florida, 1969.

NEW STUDENTS LOOK
AT CAREERS

6

The United States is the first country in the world where the number of white-collar workers has grown to exceed the number of blue-collar workers. White-collar workers constituted less than one quarter of the work force in 1910; today nearly half of all employed persons work at white-collar jobs. Not only has the last half century seen an upward shift in the occupational structure, but even within occupations there has been a spiraling demand for increased amounts and complexity of training. Workers in the professional and technical occupations now *average* more than a college education. Indeed, even clerical and sales personnel now have, on the average, more than a high school education (Borow, 1964). Education has become the gateway to the jobs of the future, and occupational preparation is a major function of postsecondary education.

When high school seniors in the SCOPE study were asked which of eight goals was the most important reason for attending college, the reason given by the largest number of people was the securing of vocational or professional training. Among entering college students participating in the American College Testing Program, 51 per cent said that their most important goal in college would be the pursuit of occupational training (Holland and Whit-

ney, 1968). An astounding 80 per cent of the freshmen entering
community colleges in the fall of 1970 agreed that "The chief benefit of a college education is that it increases one's earning power."
Across all types of colleges included in the annual ACE survey, two
thirds of the freshmen agreed with the statement (American Council on Education, 1970). Thus, whatever other claims we may make
for the importance of education, we must give the matter of career
preparation serious study. New Students, more than traditional students, look to education as the pathway to better jobs. The specific
questions to be answered in this chapter concern differences between
traditional and New Students in their concern with career development and the role that education plays in it. The relevant dimensions can be discussed under four broad headings: the processes
of making career decisions, career aspirations, career preferences,
and the characteristics of jobs rated desirable by New Students.

Making Decisions

The fewer choices one has, the easier it is to make a decision.
Applying that sweeping generalization in the area of occupational
choices, we would hypothesize that students low in traditional academic ability (low A's) will reach career decisions more readily
than high A's and that women will reach career decisions more
easily than men. The common assumption behind both predictions
is that low academic performance and female sex contribute to the
narrowing of career options. An example of the fewer career choices
available to women is provided by the Strong Vocational Interest
Blank, which measures thirty-six occupations for women and seventy-
nine for men. Levin and colleagues (1971) have noted the restric-
tion in options that accompanies the failure to obtain maximum
benefits from education. They observe the power of educational
attainment to "provide an individual with a larger number of
higher-quality alternatives from which to choose in determining his
destiny and the destiny of those in his household" (p. 3).

The data support the hypotheses that low-A students are
more likely than high-A students to have made a career choice
by the time they enter college and that women are more likely
than men to feel confident in their choice of an occupation. It follows that the subgroups of low-A women should be especially likely

to have decided upon a career by the time they enter college. And
that is a fact, according to data from both the SCOPE and CGP
samples. In both studies, low-A women were quite the most likely
subgroup to say that their occupational choice was definite. In the
SCOPE 1967 follow-up of high school seniors into college, 48 per
cent of the women who had been low-A students in high school
said that their choice of an occupation was "very definite." High-A
women were the next most likely group to have made a definite
decision (38 per cent), followed by low-A men (30 per cent) and
high-A men (26 per cent). The phrasing of the question and the
figures in the CGP sample of two-year-college entrants were different, but the pattern was identical. Thirty-two per cent of the low-A
females said that they knew exactly what kind of work they wanted
to do after finishing their education. They were followed by the
subgroup of high-A females, 22 per cent of whom were as certain
of their future occupation, followed by 18 per cent of the low-A
men and 14 per cent of the high-A men. Thus, the data tend to support the prediction that women and low-A students are the most
likely groups to have made career decisions by the time they enter
college—probably because their options are fewer.

   But an alternative explanation of the data should be considered, namely, that the closer one is to the necessity of making
a decision, the more likely it is that the decision will be made. We
could observe, for example, that low-A women will be the first subgroup to stop formal schooling to enter the labor market, whereas
high-A men have a relatively long period of time before they must
reach a definite decision about what they will do after leaving
school. In the SCOPE college sample, only 37 per cent of the low-A
women plan to attain at least a bachelor's degree, whereas 95 per
cent of the high-A men plan to remain in college for a minimum of
four years. Thus, high-A men have more time than low-A women
to reach a final career decision. But the explanation breaks down
when we observe that high-A women plan to remain in school
longer than low-A men; 89 per cent of the high-A women plan to
complete at least four years of college, compared with only 54 per
cent of the low-A men. Yet high-A women are more likely than
low-A men to have reached a career decision. The fact that most
people could predict that teaching would be the career choice of

most female college graduates is indicative of the narrow career options that have been traditionally open to women. It is not as easy to guess what career field a low-A man plans to enter. Skilled craftsman, machine operator, teacher, and foreman are all popular career choices for low-A men (SCOPE, 1966 data).

Upon entrance to college, only 16 per cent of all students feel that they will probably change their career choice; but students in two-year colleges are least likely to entertain the possibility—11 per cent, compared with 21 per cent of those in universities (American Council on Education, 1970). The experience of college, however, has some effect upon career decisions. After completing one year of college, students in the 1967 SCOPE follow-up said that college course work was the most likely of seven possible influences to affect their career goals; only 22 per cent of the low A's and 16 per cent of the high A's said that their course work had had no effect on their career plans. But courses were more likely to reinforce career choices than to change them, and there were no important differences in the extent to which courses influenced low-A and high-A students. Regarding the influence of other people on their career decisions, New Students were more likely than traditional students to attribute influence to counselors, while high A's named fellow students as a source of influence. Thirty-two per cent of the low A's and 22 per cent of the high A's credited counseling with making them more certain of their career choice; 14 per cent of the low A's and 12 per cent of the high A's said that counseling had changed their goals somewhat, and about 8 per cent of each group claimed that they were less sure (6 per cent) or had changed goals completely (2 per cent) as a result of counseling. Forty-four per cent of the low A's and 57 per cent of the high A's stated that counseling had had no effect on their career plans.

The best explanation for the greater influence of counselors on New Students probably lies in the greater availability of career counseling in community colleges; but even so, counseling has less impact on career decisions than has association with instructors. New Students and traditional students are equally influenced by instructors; most of them say that association with teachers has either reinforced their career decisions (36 per cent) or has had no effect (35 per cent). Fellow students are less likely to influence low-A students

than they are to influence high A's; 46 per cent of the low A's and
34 per cent of the high A's said that association with other students
had had no effect on career choices. But once again, where fellow
students were credited with influence, they were most likely to reinforce career choices already made. Student activities—on or off the
campus—had no effect on career goals for nearly three fourths of
the students.

In summary, the data support some broad conclusions about
the process of making career decisions: First, the more restricted the
options, the more likely it is that the student has made a career
decision. Tentatively we suggest that the limitation of choice propels
young people into career decisions more rapidly than does the nearness in time to actual employment. For example, the chances are
pretty good—better than one in three—that a female college student is preparing to become a teacher. Perhaps she plans to spend
the very minimum number of years possible in school, or perhaps
employment as a teacher is five to eight years in the future. I suggest,
however, that her decision is made because she does not perceive her
choices as numerous. Likewise, low-A students have not in the past
had the options open to them that high-A men, especially, have. The
introduction of a much broader range of career options into the
community college curriculum is beginning to broaden the vocational choices available to New Students.

Second, the sources of influence on career decisions are likely
to be related to the availability or opportunity for discussion of
careers with other people. Course work, much of which is directed
toward career preparation, exerts the greatest influence on both low-
A and high-A students, followed by association with teachers,
followed by counseling for low-A students and association with
fellow students for high A's.

Career Aspirations

Most young people expect to have more education than their
parents had, and they also expect to hold higher-status jobs. But the
influence of academic competence on career aspirations is evident in
the figures in Table 17, which shows the percentages of low-A and
high-A students from homes of fathers holding low-, middle-, or
high-status jobs. Compared with those percentages are the percent-

Table 17. FATHERS' OCCUPATIONS AND
STUDENT CAREER ASPIRATIONS

| | Job Status | | |
	Low	Middle	High
	Per Cent		
Lowest-third students			
Father's occupation	35	36	29
Own aspiration	11	41	48
Highest-third students			
Father's occupation	17	37	46
Own aspiration	1	12	86

Source: SCOPE, 1966 data.

ages representing students' own career aspirations. The shift is definitely upward for both low-A and high-A students. But the dramatic shift upward occurs for students who are successful in school. Almost all of the academically able high school seniors want to enter the professions or to become high-status white-collar workers such as managers, executives, artists, or government officials. The 12 per cent who do not aspire to the professions are mostly women who plan to be office workers. Although high-A students were more likely than low-A students to have fathers with high-status jobs, the differences in the younger generation will be much greater (38 percentage points) than the differences in the parental generation illustrated here (15 percentage points) if the occupational plans of the students come to fruition.

Lowest-third students aspire to higher-status jobs than those held by their fathers, but the steps upward are more gradual than for high-A students. Most of the low-A students who plan to enter what are classified here as high-status jobs are hoping to become social workers, teachers, and engineers—jobs that require a bachelor's degree. Middle-level jobs, desired by 41 per cent of the low-A students, include jobs such as office work, sales, and skilled crafts.

The 11 per cent who seem not to aspire much above the low-status jobs held by their fathers consist primarily of women planning to become beauticians, practical nurses, and the like.

Certainly it appears that academic achievement gives the big boost to career aspirations. Education is recognized as the path for upward mobility. The figures in Table 17 show again how important academic performance is in our society. Just as Chapter 1 showed that academic ability is the primary determinant of college attendance, so these figures show the influence of academic ability on career aspirations. A recent review of research in this area concluded that education has a significant impact on future earning power, even when ability and other intervening influences are controlled (Levin et al., 1971). Career aspirations—if they are realistic, and most of them are—are very closely related to educational aspirations. Low-A students typically choose occupations that have minimal academic requirements.

Career Preferences

Despite all the talk about the unwillingness of young people to accept the world the way it is, the evidence is that students are hard-headed realists when it comes to making career choices. Even when the SCOPE questionnaire encouraged high school seniors to dream a bit about what they would *like* to do, without thinking about what the job would pay or whether they had the necessary qualifications, most students were conservative in their desires. Low-A students tended to make occupational choices that required little in the way of advanced education. To take a vivid example, the most popular occupational choice among low-A girls was typist or secretary, both of which were selected by 78 per cent of the low-A girls, who stated that they would either like the work very much or fairly well. Top choice for low-A boys was auto mechanic, with 69 per cent of the low-A boys responding favorably.

Table 18 illustrates several patterns of occupational preferences when analyzed by academic ability and by sex. The analysis is by ability thirds—the percentage in each group responding that they would enjoy doing the work if they had the chance (stating either "I would like this very much" or "I would like this fairly well"). For the purposes of this presentation, some criteria were devised for grouping occupational preferences. For an occupational choice to appear under the heading of Category I (High Preference by Low-A Students), or Category II (High Preference by High-A Students), there had to be a large difference (minimum of 10 per cent)[1] between the percentage of low-A and high-A students responding favorably to the occupation. Second, the occupation had to be reasonably appealing to the group; at least 50 per cent of the students in the subgroup must have expressed a liking for the occupation. Thus, the occupation of typist is considered a female low-A perference because it received a favorable response from 78 per cent of the low-A girls (over half) and by only 42 per cent of the high-A girls (greater than 10 per cent differential). It is not included under any male heading, since there was no aptitude grouping where half of the men expressed an interest in doing the work of a typist. Category III (No Difference by Ability) shows those occupations that appeared almost equally attractive to all ability levels.

A number of observations may be made regarding these subsets of occupational groupings. Among the occupations of interest to low-A students there is a strong sex differentiation. Only the job of office manager appeals to both men and women. Very few low-A men say that they would enjoy typing, and very few low-A women profess an interest in auto mechanics. The situation is quite different among the choices made by high-A students. Half of the occupations that high-A students show a much greater liking for than low-A students appear on both the male and female lists. High-A women, for example, are just as interested in the work of a college president as are high-A men.

The jobs listed in Category I are stereotyped as men's jobs or women's jobs. And yet the *majority* of high-A men and women reject these jobs. More high-A men dislike auto mechanics than like it, and more high-A women dislike typing than like it. It is more accurate to speak of Category-III jobs as "women's jobs" because they have a high appeal for all women. Perhaps because of the greater variety of men's jobs, there are relatively few jobs that can be labeled "men's jobs" in the sense that they appeal to all men.

High-A females show the greatest discrepancy of all sub-

[1] With the large numbers involved in these studies, a difference of even 1 per cent is statistically significant.

Table 18. OCCUPATIONAL PREFERENCES

	Per Cent Favorable	
	Low A $N = 11,230$	High A $N = 11,728$
I. *High Preference by Low-A Students*		
A. Female Preferences		
Typist	78	42
Secretary	78	51
Office Clerk	75	37
Beautician	73	45
Store Clerk	64	39
Nurse	59	49
Office Manager	56	40
Bookkeeper	55	32
B. Male Preferences		
Auto Mechanic	69	42
Army Officer	68	53
Electrician	60	41
Office Manager	56	46
Policeman	51	32
Machinist	50	24
II. *High Preference by High-A Students*		
A. Female Preferences		
Author of Novel	60	76
High School Teacher	45	64
College Professor	33	62
College President	43	55
Doctor	38	53
Sculptor	27	50
Lab Technician	33	50
B. Male Preferences		
Author of Novel	46	59
Spaceman	46	59
College Professor	33	54
Doctor	40	53
U. S. Senator	41	53
College President	42	53

Table 18. (Cont.) OCCUPATIONAL PREFERENCES

| | Per Cent Favorable | |
	Low A $N = 11,230$	High A $N = 11,728$
III. *No Difference by Ability*		
A. Female Preferences		
Housewife	85	84
Airline Stewardess	84	79
Social Worker	79	78
Elementary Teacher	66	68
Guidance Counselor	57	60
President of		
Large Company	51	48
B. Male Preferences		
President of		
Large Company	67	71
Electrical Engineer	57	53

Source: SCOPE, 1966 data.

groups between what they would like to do and what they are likely to do. There are, for instance, very few female doctors, college professors, or college presidents. And the number of authors and sculptors is limited for either sex. At the present time, women with bachelor's degrees are considerably more likely to fill the jobs listed under Category III than they are to fill the jobs that appeal uniquely to highly able women.

The common element in Category III–A (Female Preferences) is the emphasis on working with people. The jobs do not appear to make large intellectual demands, and academic ability is probably not an important requisite for competence on the job. Low-A women are just as interested as high-A women in working as airline hostesses, social workers, or elementary school teachers—and perhaps just as capable. They are not likely to have the opportunity to do so, however, since at the present time most employers of Category-III jobs require bachelor's degrees. Thus, high-A women are generally preferred to low-A women for some of the jobs in which women of lesser academic ability are most interested.

The occupations preferred by men present in some ways a more complicated picture, perhaps because they have not been subject to as much societal stereotyping. Low-A men, for example, express a liking for jobs that require considerable specialized training. Years ago the masculine low-A jobs were physical in nature, but most of the jobs requiring physical strength have little appeal to anyone. Only 17 per cent of the men at all levels of ability, for example, expressed an interest in the work of a longshoreman. And in any case, machines have replaced physical labor; instead, highly trained technicians are needed to run the machines. Thus, low-A men are faced with some fairly complex intellectual tasks that low-A women do not face. With the exception of nursing, the female low-A job preferences do not require long periods of specialized training. The job of an auto mechanic demands considerably more training than does the job of store clerk or typist.

We might hypothesize that occupational dissatisfaction will occur most notably among low-A men and high-A women. Some low-A men may be faced with intellectual and technical demands beyond their interest or particular abilities, whereas high-A women may have interests and abilities in occupations that are not readily available to them. If jobs such as social work, guidance counseling, and elementary school teaching were not labeled "woman's work" by society, it is quite possible that some low-A men would prefer them to some of the more technical jobs of the skilled trades. There is some hard evidence to support this suggestion. Although only 37 per cent of the low-A men in the SCOPE sample of high school seniors expressed an interest in being a social worker, 67 per cent expressed an interest in helping the poor, which is certainly one of the major activities involved in social work.

When a society erects barriers to opportunity on the basis of stereotypes, those lowest in the prestige hierarchy are the recipients of snowballing restrictions on freedom of choice. Since high-A women are lower on the prestige scale than high-A men, they are displaced from Category-II jobs to Category-III jobs. For example, a woman who sees no chance to become a doctor may serve people by becoming a social worker. High-A women, however, are higher on the prestige scale than low-A women; and so they displace low-A women (who may want to be social workers, for example) from jobs in Category III. High-A women are considered better qualified for positions as social workers than low-A men, even though the relevance of academic requirements to job performance has not been demonstrated. How much better it would be if people pursued jobs that utilize their best abilities and interests instead of jobs that society deems appropriate for their sex or race.

Job Desirability

The data show some differences between traditional and New Students in job characteristics (such as salary, security, opportunity to utilize specific talents) that they regard as desirable. New Students have been widely characterized as pragmatic seekers of immediate and tangible rewards. Almost as widely touted is the characterization of today's traditional college students as selfless and socially concerned. Traditional students are supposedly rejecting big salaries and personal power in seeking jobs, and New Students are presumably interested in jobs in business and in upward mobility in the establishment. How accurate are these portrayals?

The greatest differences between traditional and New Students in job desirability occur along the dimension of money and job security. According to Project TALENT data on 1960 high school seniors, 62 per cent of the low-A students and 46 per cent of the high-A students rated a good starting income as extremely or very important. In the 1967 SCOPE sample of college freshmen, 55 per cent of the low A's and 31 per cent of the high A's felt that an opportunity to "earn a great deal of money" was essential or very important. The emphasis on tangible rewards is also illustrated by the 91 per cent of low-A college students in the 1967 SCOPE follow-up who rated job stability and security essential or very important, compared with 72 per cent of the high A's. For some not readily interpretable reason, high school seniors queried in 1960 were not as greatly concerned with job security as those in a 1967 sample; only 68 per cent of the low A's and 61 per cent of the high A's in the project TALENT sample rated "job security and permanence" as extremely or very important.

On a variety of other job characteristics, the general pattern that emerges tends to support the common belief that New Students are more concerned with tangible job rewards whereas traditional

students tend to value intangible job satisfactions. In addition to
those already discussed, the job characteristics rated essential or very
important more frequently by project TALENT low A's were freedom to make my own decisions (57 per cent of the low A's to 52
per cent of the high A's); opportunity for promotion and advance-
ment in the long run (69 per cent to 63 per cent); and meeting and
working with sociable, friendly people (71 per cent to 64 per cent).
High-A students were more likely than low-A students to stress the
necessity of doing work that seemed "important" to them (83 per
cent to 74 per cent). The pattern was similar in the 1967 SCOPE
data for college freshmen. High-A students were somewhat more
likely to value the opportunity to use special talents (42 per cent to
38 per cent) and to be creative and original (24 per cent to 20 per
cent), whereas low-A students tended to stress earnings, prestige,
and security. The interest of the low-A group in working with people
appeared in both sets of data. But the difference between the percentages of men and women expressing an interest in working with
people was greater (averaging about 20 percentage points) than
the difference between low-A and high-A groups (about nine percentage points' difference).

The data presented in this chapter verify the widely held
belief that New Students view education in pragmatic terms. Although *all* students, traditional as well as New Students, believe that
the most important functions of education lie in the general area of
occupational preparation, New Students seem especially eager to get
at the business of earning a good living. Upon entrance to college,
New Students are more likely to have made a career commitment;
they plan to concentrate on learning things that will be useful to
them in their jobs; they aspire to jobs of working with people or
things—as opposed to working with ideas or abstractions. They want
generally to have more of the good things of life than their parents
have had, and their career preferences are solidly realistic with
respect to educational requirements. Indeed, one might observe that
perhaps they are too much influenced by reality; they are much
more likely than traditional students to succumb to sex stereotyping
in job preferences. Low-A women, however, show a great deal of
interest in jobs such as social work, teaching, and guidance coun-

seling. Traditionally, these jobs have been reserved for women with college degrees, even though skills in interpersonal relations may be more relevant to good job performance than either academic prowess or sex. Perhaps the egalitarian era in higher education will force employers to look more carefully at the skills and interests of candidates and to place less emphasis on educational credentials. When all candidates have college degrees, we will have to look at what they have learned. (See Chapter 10 for further discussion.)

References

American Council on Education. *National Norms for Entering College Freshmen—Fall 1970*. ACE Research Reports, 5(6). Washington, D.C.: Office of Research, American Council on Education, 1970.

BOROW, H., (ed.). *Man in a World at Work*. Boston: Houghton Mifflin, 1964.

HOLLAND, J., AND D. R. WHITNEY. *Changes in the Vocational Plans of College Students: Orderly or Random?* ACT Research Report, No. 25. Iowa City: American College Testing Program, April 1968.

LEVIN, H. M., GUTHRIE, J. W., KLEINDORFER, G. B., AND STOUT, R. T. "School Achievement and Post-School Success: A Review." *Review of Educational Research, 41*(1), 1971.

BEYOND HIGH SCHOOL: NEW STUDENTS AS ADULTS

7

The topic that is the subject of this book is, for the most part, necessarily future-oriented. New Students are just beginning to present challenges to postsecondary education and to the broader society. We do not have much experience to draw upon in facing the prospect of universal higher education. But we do have some miniexperiences. We know of individual students who conform to the research description of New Students—at least superficially—who have attended college in the past. We know that some institutions of postsecondary education have for many years catered to a clientele that consists of nontraditional college students. Fortunately, we even have some data on the outcomes of education—and the outcomes of lack of education.

How handicapping is limited education in a society that places education on a pedestal? How well have various kinds of educational experiences prepared young people to cope with the demands of life in the twentieth century? Can a person born in poverty escape it through education? Is education as important to future career status as we have been led to believe? Some insights bearing on these important questions are available in the massive data bank of Project TALENT. In seeking answers to the questions posed, I distilled bits of information from the profiles of 20,965 young men and women who met three criteria: (1) They had participated as high school seniors in the full research program of Project TALENT in 1960. (2) They had participated in *both* the one-year follow-up in 1961 and in the five-year follow-up in 1965. (3) They were working full time in 1965. The bias of the sample lies in the cooperativeness of the young people; only remarkably cooperative people are included in these analyses. They not only had to stay with the study for five years, but they had to furnish *all* of the information needed to answer the particular question under study.

Educational Attainment and Salary

The first question asked of the data was "How much difference does postsecondary education make in the amount of salary received five years after high school graduation?" The answer is that it made a lot of difference in the mid 1960s. A student with a bachelor's degree who was just entering his first year of work experience was likely to make more money than a young person who had had five years of experience in the labor market but no postsecondary education. Table 19 illustrates the monetary value of a college degree. In this analysis a salary of $400 per month was selected as a typical salary for a person in his early twenties in 1965. Forty-five per cent of the male and 36 per cent of the female full-time workers in the TALENT study reported salaries of over $400 per month, making the figure a somewhat better than average salary.

The groups shown in Table 19 consist of all possible combinations of "highs" and "lows" on each of three variables. The highs on postsecondary education are those who had obtained a bachelor's degree by 1965; the lows are those who had received no certification of any schooling beyond high school. The highs on academic aptitude (high A) consist of those who scored in the top third of TALENT 1960 high school senior norms on the academic-aptitude composite, whereas the lows are those who scored in the lowest third. The highs and lows on socioeconomic status (SES) are those who ranked in the top or bottom third among high school seniors on the

Table 19. FULL-TIME WORKERS REPORTING SALARIES OF
MORE THAN $400 PER MONTH IN 1965
(FIVE YEARS AFTER HIGH SCHOOL GRADUATION)

			Male	Female
			Per Cent	
1 Bachelor's Degree	High A ...	High SES	71	70
2 Bachelor's Degree	High A ...	Low SES	69	65
3 Bachelor's Degree	Low A ...	High SES	65	62
4 Bachelor's Degree	Low A ...	Low SES	55	36
5 No Postsecondary Ed. .	High A ...	High SES	48	24
6 No Postsecondary Ed. .	Low A ...	High SES	40	19
7 No Postsecondary Ed. .	High A ...	Low SES	36	18
8 No Postsecondary Ed. .	Low A ...	Low SES	26	6

Source: Special analysis of Project TALENT data.

TALENT socioeconomic index. Table 19 shows the percentages of the sixteen subgroups who were making more than $400 per month for full-time work in 1965. The range is from 71 per cent of the men in group 1 to 6 per cent of the women in group 8.

The percentages in Table 19 are based on data for 5,531 young men and women—the number remaining after elimination of those falling in "middle" categories on academic ability, SES, education, and salary, plus all of those lacking *any* item of information necessary for the four-way classification scheme used. As might be expected, groups 1 and 8 were the largest in size numerically—illustrating once again the tendency of the world to divide into two groups—the "haves" and the "have-nots." Most young people from privileged homes made high test scores, graduated from college, and made above-average salaries. Most young people from poor homes made low test scores, took no formal education beyond high school, and made low salaries. But the data also show the power of education to change the status of young people.

The possession of a bachelor's degree has more influence on

salary than any other characteristic measured. College graduates, regardless of ability or SES, make higher salaries than those without postsecondary education. All bachelor's degree subgroups (groups 1–4) rank above all no-postsecondary-education groups (groups 5–8). To determine the effectiveness of a college degree in producing a relatively good salary, compare two groups of men who are comparable in academic promise and socioeconomic background—for example, groups 1 and 5. The only difference between these two groups on our measures is that the men in group 1 have a college degree and those in group 5 do not. Whereas 71 per cent of the college-degree men were making above-average salaries, only 48 per cent of the nondegree men of comparable ability and background were in this income bracket. Approximately the same discrepancy exists between the salaries of degree and nondegree men in subgroups 4 and 8. Low-A–low-SES men who managed to make it through college (numerically only 59, compared to 699 who did not) were twice as likely as their noncollege peers to be making better than average salaries in 1965.

One might well inquire what personal qualities were present in those few men of low SES and low measured ability who managed not only to enter college but to obtain their degrees. One might be just as curious about the motivations of men with high ability *and* high SES (group 5) who stopped all formal education upon receipt of a high school diploma. The very existence of these atypical groups reminds us that personal characteristics play an important role in aspirations and achievements at all of the choice points in the lives of individuals. It is, of course, highly likely that the same personal qualities that lead a person to enter college also contribute heavily to the probability that he will remain in college to graduate and that he will seek a good job and be promoted rapidly. Nevertheless, extensive research on the subject does show that some portion of the monetary benefits of the college degree is attributable to higher educational attainment alone (Levin et al., 1971). There have been numerous attempts to tease out of research data the proportion of the income differential between college graduates and those who have not attended college that can be attributed to the mere possession of the degree. There is more consensus among researchers than one might suspect, and a review of the available data suggests that the "percentage of income differential directly due to schooling is somewhere between 67 and 82 per cent" (Hartnett, 1971, p. E-6). Next to educational attainment, academic ability is the important determiner of income for those competing for high-level jobs, while socioeconomic background is the more important influence in the salary competition among lower-level jobs. Notice that high-A college graduates make more money than low-A college graduates regardless of the background of their parents. These data are in agreement with those reported by Spaeth and Greeley (1970), which led to their conclusion that among college graduates the ability of the student had roughly four times more to do with the prestige of his job seven years after college graduation than did the socioeconomic standing of his parents. Among students represented in Table 19 who quit their formal education upon high school graduation, however, the situation was just the opposite. Those from high-SES homes made higher salaries than those from low-SES backgrounds regardless of ability. In other words, it looks as though education is a very important and realistic pathway to higher economic status. Young people who do not participate in formal education beyond high school remain in the same relative socioeconomic position as their parents, whereas low-SES youth who pursue further education have more chance of advancing on the basis of ability. Low-SES students had a good chance in 1960 of raising their socioeconomic position through higher education.

While salary *patterns* are similar for men and women, salary *figures* are not. Note that college makes much more difference to women's salaries than to men's. Salaries of women with a college degree compare favorably with those of men—at least until the low-A–low-SES group. Women without education beyond high school have only about half the probability of comparable men for good salaries. Actually, college women do not fare quite so well financially as this table indicates. Although they do tend to equal the men in making salaries of $400 or more per month, very few of them make high salaries. For example, whereas 23 per cent of the men in subgroup 1 made over $600 per month, only 4 per cent of the comparable group of women did. Almost half of subgroup-1 women fell in the salary range of $400 to $500 per month.

All of the observations made about the data in Table 19

support the notion that higher education was an effective device for achieving upward mobility—at least as it is measured financially—in the 1960 to 1965 time period, when a relatively small proportion of the population had college degrees. The situation is changing rapidly, however. Theoretically at least, true egalitarian higher education would eradicate the financial advantage of a college degree. When everyone has one, decisions about whom to hire and promote will have to be determined by other criteria. What does this mean for New Students? It may mean that while their absolute standard of living rises, their position in society *relative* to their high-A classmates will remain unchanged. The argument would go something like this.

When 80 per cent of all high school students go on to college, the 20 per cent who do not will have a serious occupational handicap; at the same time, those who go to college will find that the possession of a degree gives them no advantage over 80 per cent of their competition. As Hartnett (1971) puts it, "Young people, it seems, will have everything to lose if they don't go to college, but very little to gain if they do" (p. E-10). Furthermore, the data in Table 19, as well as those presented by Spaeth and Greeley (1970), show that when the factor of a college education is held constant (as in groups 1–4 of Table 19), ability becomes the major determinant of salary. If that situation remains the same in the 1970s, the relative position of New Students in the salary hierarchy will remain unchanged—even though more of them will have college educations. In other words, egalitarian higher education does not necessarily herald the dawning of an egalitarian society. As a matter of fact, it is likely to lead to a more sharply delineated meritocracy. Workers will advance according to their ability, and both educational attainment and family SES will decline in importance—except insofar as they actually contribute to the individual's ability to perform the jobs that have high salaries attached to them.

Educational Attainment and Job Satisfaction

Salary is only one dimension of job success; many young people today appear to be rejecting the success criterion of salary in favor of defining vocational success in terms of personal satisfaction. Table 20 indicates the relationship between educational attainment and job satisfaction. For the data shown here, young people five years out of high school were asked how they felt about their present type of work. Any one of five responses, ranging from "very satisfied" to "very dissatisfied," could be made. Table 20 shows the percentages in each subgroup who said they were "very satisfied" with their work.

When the measure of job success is satisfaction, the possession of a college degree still apparently results in an occupational

Table 20. FULL-TIME WORKERS "VERY SATISFIED" WITH THEIR WORK FIVE YEARS AFTER HIGH SCHOOL GRADUATION

	MEN			Per Cent
1	Bachelor's Degree	Low A	... Low SES	63
2	Bachelor's Degree	Low A	... High SES	60
3	Bachelor's Degree	High A	... Low SES	52
4	Bachelor's Degree	High A	... High SES	51
5	No Postsecondary Ed.	Low A	... High SES	49
6	No Postsecondary Ed.	Low A	... Low SES	44
7	No Postsecondary Ed.	High A	... Low SES	40
8	No Postsecondary Ed.	High A	... High SES	40
	WOMEN			
1	Bachelor's Degree	Low A	... High SES	76
2	Bachelor's Degree	High A	... High SES	62
3	Bachelor's Degree	High A	... Low SES	62
4	No Postsecondary Ed.	Low A	... High SES	61
5	No Postsecondary Ed.	High A	... High SES	57
6	Bachelor's Degree	Low A	... Low SES	55
7	No Postsecondary Ed.	Low A	... Low SES	53
8	No Postsecondary Ed.	High A	... Low SES	50

Source: Analysis of Project TALENT data.

advantage. For men, those with college degrees derived more satisfaction from their work than those who had no formal education beyond high school. But there is an important difference between the order of groups in Tables 19 and 20. Whereas high-A college men made the highest salaries, low-A college men expressed the greatest satisfaction with their work. Likewise, low-A nondegree men were better satisfied than their high-A counterparts, who also had no education beyond high school.

Throughout these and other studies, there is a consistent tendency for high A's to be less easily satisfied than low A's. The phenomenon is especially apparent at the present time among the highly critical campus activists, who tend to be among the brightest and most articulate of young people. The apparent job satisfaction of low A's may be primarily the result of a combination of the lower job aspirations and greater tendency toward acquiescence on the part of low A's when compared with high A's.

The same two tendencies may also help to account for the higher percentages of expressed job satisfaction among women. Even though there is widespread agreement that able young women are underemployed, more women on the whole say that they are satisfied with their jobs than men do. Many young women in this age bracket may be working at low-level jobs that they regard as temporary until they marry or have children. In these cases, they may aspire to little more than pleasant working conditions, making the discrepancy between aspirations and reality comfortably small. The only group that is really out of logical order in Table 20 is the low-A–low-SES group of women with college degrees. This is the same group that appeared somewhat out of place in the salary data illustrated in Table 19, in that a substantial number of these women were making low salaries. This group is of considerable interest because the students in it represent the advance guard of New Students; although these students were low-A and low-SES, they had received bachelor's degrees by 1965. Perhaps the best explanation for the fairly poor showing of these women on the dimension of job success—financially and in personal satisfaction—is that the groups with which they are compared are high-A college graduates of both sexes and low-A college men. It has been observed that discrimination—although it may not present great handicaps for highly able persons—is at its worst for minority people who are average or below in ability (see Chapter 9). In the competition for jobs calling for college degrees, these women are at a clear disadvantage to men with college degrees as well as to more able women. Viewed from another perspective, it is not especially surprising that high-SES females without college degrees (groups 4 and 5) should express relatively high satisfaction with their jobs. These high-SES women undoubtedly have personal characteristics that create a demand for their services as receptionists, secretaries, and other relatively high-status female occupations requiring middle- and upper-class social amenities.

Perspectives on Decision-Making

One of the important sources of information that should prove useful in improving education for New Students is the perspective of their predecessors as they look back on their educational experiences. The Project TALENT staff asked young people five years out of high school to indicate which major decisions they regretted. Most of the alternatives offered were related to decisions regarding postsecondary education. Table 21 shows the percentage in each subgroup responding that they were *not* sorry about any important decisions that they had made.

Aptitude standing is clearly *the* important factor in determining satisfaction with past decisions. It is only *within* the aptitude groupings that SES has influence—and then in the expected direction. That is, higher SES permits one to make better decisions, other things being equal. When satisfactions with particular decisions are examined, it is apparent that many answers are limited by what the person actually did. For example, low-A–low-SES students are the most likely group to wish that they had taken additional educational training after high school to prepare for a better job, whereas high-A–high-SES students were most likely to wish that they had chosen a different major field in college. It is interesting that there is no variation at all among groups in the level of satisfaction with non-education-related matters such as vocational choice and age of marriage. Ten to 12 per cent were unhappy about these decisions regardless of aptitude or SES background. Women, however, were just about twice as likely as men to regret marrying at an early age,

Table 21. STUDENTS EXPRESSING SATISFACTION WITH
IMPORTANT DECISIONS MADE

	Males	Females
	Per Cent	
High A—High SES	69	67
High A—Low SES	59	63
Middle A—High SES	55	62
Middle A—Middle SES	52	61
Middle A—Low SES	48	59
Low A—High SES	48	54
Low A—Low SES	42	54

Source: Reanalysis of Project TALENT data.

with the lower-A and lower-SES groups expressing the greatest regret—again probably because they were the ones to marry young.

Education Evaluated

The two most frequently cited purposes of education are to prepare the student for a vocation and to add to the general enrichment of life. As students look back from a perspective five years beyond high school, they appear fairly well satisfied with education on both counts. Over all levels of ability and educational attainment, half of the students said that their training and education had prepared them "very well" (the top choice offered) for a full life outside their work; 40 per cent were equally enthusiastic about their education as preparation for a vocation. Surely these figures will surprise many who have been critical of education's vocational emphasis. Students themselves—from a perspective of five years out of high school—feel better prepared for participating in a full life than for a vocation that will make full use of their abilities. Since it is difficult for any of us to say just what education can or should do to help bring about a "full and satisfying" life, it is hard to know how or where or whether to fault education when life is not full and satisfying.

Table 22 shows the percentages of students with various types of postsecondary educational experiences who could be described as very well satisfied with their education.

As the Project TALENT students see it, the more education they have, the better prepared they are for living a full life. And this feeling has implications for our national goal of universal higher education; college graduates are more likely to rate their educational background as very good preparation for life than are those who have taken no study beyond high school. The same general pattern emerged for students' evaluation of their vocational preparation, with one interesting exception. Women who had received a license or certificate of some kind—business school, nursing, beauty school—were the most likely group of all to feel that their vocational education had prepared them to make full use of their abilities. Fifty-four per cent rated their training very good, compared with 47 per cent for the college graduates.

There is some logic to the conclusion that a curriculum established for the single purpose of training for a vocation *should* result in greater student satisfaction on this dimension. It does for the women, but not for the men. The men's rate of satisfaction with education for a vocation follows the same pattern as that for a preparation for a full and satisfying life. The more education they have, the better prepared they feel. We can only speculate about the reasons for the differences between men and women with regard to the popularity of specific vocational training offered by licensing curricula. Men's careers are likely to be greatly influenced by their educational *credentials*. Women's careers are not so educationally sensitive—at least not among those women receiving some form of postsecondary education. In most large offices, for example, one can find secretaries with high school diplomas, business school certificates, and junior college and four-year college degrees. There are even a few with graduate degrees. One would be hard put to find such a wide range of educational backgrounds among men in a single job category. The more education a man has, the greater his career opportunities. Certainly, the same could not be said for women in the 1960–65 time period. Therefore, women with specific vocational training probably had jobs that made better use of their

Table 22. STUDENTS RATING EDUCATION "VERY GOOD" FOR LATER LIFE

| | Level of Postsecondary Education | | | | |
| | None N = 8,350 | License N = 4,642 | J.C. N = 873 | B.A. N = 9,361 | Total N = 23,226 |
	Per Cent	Per Cent	Per Cent	Per Cent	Per Cent
For Full Life					
Male	38	39	42	54	46
Female	46	54	53	64	54
				—	—
					50
For Satisfying Occupation					
Male	25	31	36	44	35
Female	35	54	45	47	44
				—	—
					40

Source: Special Analysis of Project TALENT data.

abilities than those with more general two- or four-year liberal-arts backgrounds.

The lack of enthusiasm of college-educated women who were working full time in 1965 is more evident than it first appears in the figures presented in Table 22. Women generally tend to be more positive than men on ratings, and the figures in Table 22 show that they gave favorable ratings to their educations at a rate roughly 10 per cent higher than the men. But on the rating of the vocational preparation of trade schools, they were 23 per cent higher. The difference between male and female four-year-college graduates who were well satisfied with the vocational preparation was lowest of all—a mere 3 per cent. These figures tend to support the interpretation that college probably does not prepare women well to use their abilities in a vocation. Improvement of this situation undoubtedly lies with education, society, employers, and women themselves. It is likely to become an important question as careers outside the home become increasingly important in women's lives.

The years of the 1960s were good years in which to observe the impact of education upon the lives of young people. The data show that postsecondary education—the credentials, the experience, or both—was a considerable advantage to the individuals fortunate enough to participate in it. Increasing amounts of education are associated with higher salaries, greater job satisfaction, fewer regrets about the major decisions made in life, and greater feelings of confidence in achieving a full and satisfying life.

Despite those strong arguments for universal higher education, there are reasons for questioning the assumption that a straight-line extrapolation of the data leads inevitably to the conclusion that more education for more people will result in a better society and happier citizens. In the first place, the relative economic value of a college degree will decrease when everyone has one. Second, the evidence indicates that college graduates with higher *academic* ability are likely to make more money, be better satisfied with their decisions, and lead a more satisfying life than those of lower academic ability. There is little likelihood that New Students will beat traditional students at their own game, that relative ability standings will change; and hence there is little reason to think that the academic meritocracy will topple when everyone goes to college. Third, there is evidence that morale is based upon *relative* positions—not upon absolute standards. The research on the morale of soldiers in World War II (Stouffer et al., 1949) showed that everyone was much happier when the promotion was only 30 per cent of a group compared to a promotion rate of 60 per cent. At 30 per cent, those who made it thought it an honor, while the 70 per cent that didn't could see that most people were like themselves. But with a 60 per cent promotion rate, those who made it thought it a minor recognition because so many others made it, while those who were not promoted could not take refuge in numbers. Fourth, Berg (1970) has presented convincing evidence that a growing number of workers are already overeducated for their jobs, and his conclusion is borne out by the relative dissatisfaction of college-educated women shown in the data presented herein.

More of the same, then, is not enough. The *development* of individual talent should be the goal of education. The *use* of talent should be a goal of a healthy society. Education needs to take a careful look at individual differences and at new methods for fulfilling individual potential. The world of work needs to depart from dependence on credentials and to provide a more appropriate match between worker characteristics and job requirements.

References

BERG, I. *Education and Jobs: The Great Training Robbery.* Prepared for the Center for Urban Education. New York: Praeger, 1970.

HARTNETT, R. T. *Universal Higher Education: For Whose Benefit?* A Paper Prepared for the Select Education Subcommittee of the Education and Labor Committee of the House of Representatives. Princeton: Educational Testing Service, 1971.

LEVIN, H. M., GUTHRIE, J. W., KLEINDORFER, G. B., AND STOUT, R. T. "School Achievement and Post-School Success: A Review." *Review of Educational Research, 41*(1), 1971.

SPAETH, J. L., AND A. M. GREELEY. *Recent Alumni and Higher Education.* A General Report Prepared for the Carnegie Commission on Higher Education. New York: McGraw-Hill, 1970.

STOUFFER, S., SUCHMAN, E., DE VINNEY, L., STAR, S., AND WILLIAMS, R. *The American Soldier: Adjustment during Army Life,* Vol. I. Princeton: Princeton University Press, 1949.

ETHNIC MINORITIES AS NEW STUDENTS

8

Race has been and continues to be one of the major barriers to higher education. Membership in an ethnic minority group, frequently coupled with low family income, low parental occupational and educational status, poor school achievement, and low test scores, has posed a near-insurmountable barrier to college for thousands of young people.

The order of the college-attendance rates for the various ethnic minorities is very difficult to establish with any degree of precision. It depends heavily upon the regional and urban/rural representation in the sample. About the only thing that can be said with confidence is that studies generally agree that Caucasians and Orientals are much more likely to enter college than are American Indians, Spanish Americans, Negroes, or Puerto Ricans. Nevertheless, it may prove helpful to look at the data from a given sample. Among 1969 SCOPE seniors, classified by ethnic group, 61 per cent of the Caucasians and only 40 per cent of the non-Caucasians entered some form of postsecondary education in the fall following their graduation from high school. The lowest rate was found among American Indians, only 30 per cent of whom continued formal education after high school. Black Americans had the next-lowest rate

(37 per cent), followed by Spanish Americans (42 per cent), those of mixed minority backgrounds (45 per cent), and Orientals (50 per cent).[1] Since the dropout rate from high school is greater for ethnic minorities than for whites, the situation is even worse than it appears in these figures, which compare only those who actually graduated from high school. The situation is especially serious among American Indians and black Americans in the SCOPE sample.

Some of the differential in the educational attainments of whites and nonwhites can be attributed to the depressed occupational levels of ethnic minorities in this country. For example, there are not very many black professionals or executives. Table 23 shows the job levels of the fathers of the 1969 SCOPE high school seniors. Included among those classified as non-Caucasians are students who identified themselves as Negro, Indian, Spanish American, Oriental, or of mixed ethnic backgrounds.

Whereas about half of the Caucasians fall into the blue-collar occupational categories labeled "low" and "moderate," 81 per cent of the fathers of blacks are blue-collar workers. The occupational category labeled "very high," professionals and executives, includes 21 per cent of the whites and only 7 per cent of the blacks.

Even at the *same* job levels, young people belonging to ethnic minority groups are less likely to continue formal education. Among minority youth whose fathers have managed to make it into the professions against great odds, the rate of college attendance is not as high as for white students; 75 per cent of the children of white professionals continue their education, compared with 58 per cent for the children of black professionals.

Socioeconomic Status

The low socioeconomic status (SES) of ethnic minority families is so well known that documentation hardly seems necessary. But because SES and academic ability play vital roles in college attendance, a brief review of some of the data as they affect college

[1] Although the *order* of the ethnic groups in the SCOPE sample is similar to those reported in other studies, the actual figures are probably low. National figures for entrance into postsecondary education are closer to 70 per cent than the 56 per cent reported for the four-state SCOPE sample.

Table 23. OCCUPATIONAL LEVELS OF THE FATHERS OF SCOPE
HIGH SCHOOL SENIORS IN 1969

| | | Ethnic Status | |
Father's Occupational Level	Caucasian	Non-Caucasian	Black
	Per Cent	*Per Cent*	*Per Cent*
Low	21	37	45
Moderate	32	35	36
High	27	18	12
Very High	21	10	7

Source: SCOPE 1969 data analysis by Tillery and Associates.

attendance may prove useful in grasping the magnitude of the problem. Knoell (1970) found that the differences in SES between blacks and whites in her sample were so great that it was difficult to find categories that were functional for both groups. For example, in Dallas and Philadelphia she found that about one fourth of the blacks in the lowest socioeconomic category were attending college; but she was unable to compare this rate with the rate for whites, simply because an insufficient number of whites were in that very low income bracket. In Dallas, Fort Worth, and Philadelphia, two thirds to four fifths of the whites in the highest SES categories were attending college; but comparison of these figures with college-attendance rates for high-SES blacks was not possible because there were so few blacks in the highest income groups.

Blacks who do enter college do so against considerable socioeconomic odds. In a nationwide survey involving some 243,000 college freshmen, 12,300 of whom were black, Bayer and Boruch (1969) found that 56 per cent of the blacks and only 14 per cent of the nonblacks (all of those who did not check "Negro" on the item requesting racial background) were from homes in which the parental income was less than $6,000 per year in 1968. Over half of the fathers of college blacks had not completed high school, while about a quarter of the nonblacks came from homes of equally low academic accomplishment. Black college freshmen were twice as likely to come from blue-collar families (48 per cent from the ranks of skilled, semiskilled, or unskilled workers) as were nonblacks (25 per cent). Given those indices of financial resources, it is to be expected that nearly three times as many blacks (21 per cent) as nonblacks (8 per cent) expressed major concern about financing their education. Of necessity, blacks were much more likely than nonblacks to get major financial support from scholarships, grants, and loans during their freshman year, whereas nonblacks tended to derive financial support from parents and from personal savings.

Educational Aspirations

In spite of substantial socioeconomic handicaps, research shows that there is a great desire for education on the part of most minority students and their parents. Nonwhites, to a greater extent than whites, see college as the principal avenue to upward mobility, and their perception of the importance of education clearly corresponds to reality. Brimmer (1969) cites evidence to show that over the past decade the income of college-educated black males has been increasing almost twice as fast as for whites. This does not mean that higher education has closed the wide salary gaps between blacks and whites with the same educational credentials; but college degrees in the hands of minority youth are narrowing the income differences.

Minority youth, as a group, have high aspirations for college educations. Table 24 shows the plans of high school seniors of the class of 1965, as reported in U.S. Bureau of Census data. The difference between the college aspirations of whites and nonwhites (all ethnic minorities) is less than that between males and females. Sixty-seven per cent of the nonwhites were considering college—either "maybe" or "definitely"—in 1965, compared with 60 per cent of the whites. Once students are enrolled in college, the high educational goals of ethnic minorities continue to be manifest. Approximately 55 per cent of the blacks and 42 per cent of the nonblacks who were college freshmen in 1968 said they were planning postbaccalaureate work (Bayer and Boruch, 1969). Yet without considerable change in the college access routes, the aspirations of many minority youth are destined to be unrealized.

Table 25 shows the college plans of Caucasians and all other high school seniors by verbal aptitude. At the high levels of ability there is little difference between the aspirations of Caucasian and minority youth. Over 80 per cent of those—Caucasian or minority—with above-average verbal scores plan some college work. Knoell (1970) found, however, that at high levels of ability blacks were less likely to enroll in college than whites of the same ability level. In four of the five cities in her study, the rate of college attendance for highly able whites exceeded that for equally able blacks by an average rate of about 10 per cent.

On the other hand, an exceptionally large number of minority youth with very low verbal ability apparently plan exten-

Table 24. COLLEGE PLANS OF HIGH SCHOOL SENIORS (1965)

Senior Plans	Male	Female	White	Nonwhite
	Per Cent		*Per Cent*	
No college	21	37	30	20
Don't know about college	11	10	10	13
College: "Yes, maybe"	28	22	24	30
Two-year college only	9	8	9	8
Four-year college	19	14	15	21
College: "Yes, definitely"	40	31	36	37
Two-year college only	5	5	5	7
Four-year college	35	26	31	30

Source: Unpublished tabulation by A. J. Jaffee and Walter Adams of a special survey conducted by the U.S. Bureau of the Census (presented in Froomkin, 1969).

sive higher education. Sixty-three per cent of the minority students and 39 per cent of the majority youth with very low levels of verbal ability say that they plan at least to enter college. At the present time, it is highly unlikely that anywhere near 63 per cent of the minority youth with very low test scores will get to college, suffering as many do from the multiple handicaps of minority ethnic membership, low SES, and low academic ability. There is some evidence, however,

Table 25. COLLEGE PLANS OF HIGH SCHOOL SENIORS BY VERBAL
ABILITY (1965)

Level of Verbal Ability	No College	Less Than Four Years	More Than Four Years	Four Years
	Per Cent	Per Cent	Per Cent	Per Cent
Very low				
Caucasian	61	24	11	4
Non-Caucasian	37	32	21	10
Low to average				
Caucasian	43	23	25	9
Non-Caucasian	28	25	27	19
Above average				
Caucasian	18	12	39	30
Non-Caucasian	17	11	33	38

Source: Adapted from special tabulations of the Coleman twelfth-grade data, reported by Walter Adams, "Caste and Class, Relative Deprivation, and Higher Education" (presented in Froomkin, 1969).

that in the low ranges of traditionally measured academic achievement, blacks are as likely as nonblacks, if not somewhat more likely, to enroll in college. Across all of the postsecondary institutions in the ACE survey (Bayer and Boruch, 1969), 42 per cent of the enrolled black freshmen reported high school grades of $C+$ or lower, compared to 24 per cent of the nonblacks; in universities the differences in high school grades of black and white enrolled freshmen were also quite substantial—the percentages were 33 per cent to 20 per cent respectively. In predominantly white two-year colleges, however, the high school grade-point average of black and nonblack students was fairly similar; 59 per cent of the blacks and 53 per cent of the nonblacks reported high school grades of $C+$ or below. In the Knoell (1970) data, blacks with low test scores enter college at about the same rate as whites in the same score range.

In a thought-provoking article in the *New York Times Magazine* (December 13, 1970) black economist Thomas Sowell claimed that many selective colleges are passing over well-qualified blacks in favor of "obviously unqualified ones" in the search for "authentic ghetto types." Part of the trouble, he observes, is that "Often intellectually oriented black students are *defined* as middle class in outlook, whatever their actual social origins." If this charge is true, the practice of seeking blacks with low test scores would, of course, maximize academic differences between white and black students at selective institutions.

The hope for higher education is certainly evident in the expressed aspirations of minority youth and their parents. Despite the fact that few nonwhite mothers have attended college themselves, they are more likely than white mothers to desire college for their children. In data collected in a census survey, 61 per cent of the white mothers wanted at least a four-year degree for their children, compared to 67 per cent of the nonwhite mothers (Froomkin, 1969). The observation has been made many times that education is the pathway out of the cycle of poverty for many thousands of minority youth. It seems to be the opportunities that are lacking; it is certainly not the aspirations.

Academic Ability

One of the most difficult barriers to higher education for members of minority ethnic groups, however, has been low test scores and low academic performance. In a meritocratic era, in which college admission is determined by test scores and grades, the barriers imposed by the conditions of poverty homes and poverty schools have proved formidable for minority youth of college age.

Table 26 presents median test scores of various ethnic groups as reported in the well-known Coleman study (1966). With regard to the test data the researchers note:

These tests do not measure intelligence, nor attitudes, nor qualities of character. Furthermore, they are not, nor are they intended to be, "culture-free." Quite the reverse: they are culture-bound. What they measure are the skills, which are among the most important in our society, for getting a good job and moving up to a

Table 26. NATIONWIDE MEDIAN TEST SCORES OF TWELFTH-GRADE PUPILS

Test	Puerto Ricans	Indian Americans	Mexican Americans	Oriental Americans	Negro	Majority
	Per Cent	*Per Cent*	*Per Cent*	*Per Cent*	*Per Cent*	*Per Cent*
Nonverbal	43.3	47.1	45.0	51.6	40.9	52.0
Verbal	43.1	43.7	43.8	49.6	40.9	52.1
Reading	42.6	44.3	44.2	48.8	42.2	51.9
Mathematics	43.7	45.9	45.5	51.3	41.8	51.8
General information	41.7	44.7	43.3	49.0	40.6	52.2
Average of the five tests	43.1	45.1	44.4	50.1	41.1	52.0

Source: Coleman, 1966.

better one, and full participation in an increasingly technical world. Consequently, a pupil's test results at the end of public school provide a good measure of the range of opportunities open to him as he finishes school—a wide range of choice of jobs or colleges if these skills are very high; a very narrow range that includes only the most menial jobs if these skills are very low [p. 20].

The Coleman report found that minority children fell further and further behind white children as they progressed through the school system.

For most minority groups, then, and most particularly the Negro, schools provide no opportunity at all for them to overcome this initial deficiency; in fact, they fall further behind the white majority in the development of several skills which are critical to making a living and participating fully in modern society. Whatever may be the combination of nonschool factors—poverty, community attitudes, low educational level of parents—which put minority children at a disadvantage in verbal and nonverbal skills when they enter the first grade, the fact is the schools have not overcome it [p. 20].

By the time minority youth reach college age, the multiple disadvantages of their past opportunities for academic learning are fully apparent. Kendrick (1967–68) estimates that between 10 and 15 per cent of black high school seniors would score 400 or more on the verbal section of the SAT and only 2 per cent would score as high as 500. (Mean score for 1969 SAT candidates on the verbal portion was 457.) Knoell (1970) found few blacks scoring high on various traditional academic tests in the five cities in which she studied the barriers to college attendance for black youth. The percentages scoring in the highest ability group ranged from 7 per cent (compared to 51 per cent of the whites) in a southern city to 13 per cent (compared to 32 per cent of the whites) in a northern city. In the CGP sample of junior college students from forty-five colleges, all minority groups scored lower than Caucasians on a test of verbal and grammatical skills. The percentages in the lowest two fifths of the total group were as follows: Caucasian, 29 per cent; American Indian, 54 per cent; Oriental, 62 per cent; Mexican American, 63 per cent; Negro, 71 per cent. (A description of the sample and criterion test can be found in Appendix B—CGP.)

Problems of Testing

Although poor test scores and failure to attend college are closely related, the question of whether they are indicative of poor performance in college depends on a number of things. The extent to which the test taps the critical skills required in the classroom is probably the most important predictor of college performance. Tests have been criticized for relying too heavily on verbal ability, but test makers have learned that most academic curricula are heavily dependent on verbal skills and that the work sample of the test will predict the real situation only if it is as similar as possible to the conditions of the classroom. Tests are verbally loaded because college classrooms are verbally loaded. The nearly exclusive reliance of the schools on lectures and books as primary sources of learning penalizes those whose backgrounds have not emphasized learning through these media, and educators should feel a deep obligation to discover and use a variety of methods that promote learning for students of differing backgrounds and experiences. In like manner, the development of measures of varied learning styles should be a matter of first priority for testing specialists. This does not mean that nonverbal tests or nonverbal curricula are the simple answer. Contrary to popular opinion, there is evidence to indicate that when nonverbal spatial tests have been used, in the belief that they are "culture fair," the differences in scores between whites and blacks are even greater than on verbal tests (Flaugher, 1970).

Another factor that affects the predictability of academic performance is the test environment. If, for example, the student is tense and anxious, not feeling well, antagonistic toward the test situation or the test administrator, his scores will not indicate what he could do under more favorable circumstances. Katz (1970) found that when black students thought their probability of success on a test was high, the best performance was achieved when the test administrator was white. Presumably, the subjects tried harder under these conditions. But when black youth felt that the probability of success was low (as they did when they were told that they would be compared against white norms), the use of a black test administrator was likely to yield far better test performance. These findings have considerable importance for test administration; but beyond that, they have profound implications for increased understanding about the effects of expectations of failure or success by minority youth in academic competition. (See Chapter 2 for a comprehensive discussion of this issue.)

The important question of test-speededness has not been adequately researched. Although speed of learning is all too frequently associated with quality of learning (see Riessman, 1962), speed is likely to assume more importance in the test situation than in the classroom. We know that slow workers are penalized by the usual aptitude test, but we do not know whether this practice results in a *biased* test score. A speeded test (one that many students fail to finish) probably would not be a very accurate predictor of grades in a classroom where the student could proceed at his own pace, but in most classes the fast worker usually produces more and is rewarded with higher grades by teachers. To the extent that a speeded test reflects an emphasis on speed in the classroom (even though such emphasis is unjustified), the test would tend to be unbiased.

Another factor in the test environment that has been given little attention in research on test bias is the instructions given about guessing on the test. The cautious student who is afraid to give a wrong answer will make a score that may represent an underestimate of what he knows about the subject. Since there is evidence that the school situation has instilled a fear-of-failure approach to learning for many low achievers (see Chapter 2), the question of guessing would seem to be a fertile and unplowed field for further research. Students who fear giving a wrong answer on a test will be penalized more heavily than those who are willing to guess, because some of the guesses will prove correct.

Many research studies have investigated ethnic bias in traditional admissions tests, and the great weight of the evidence is that the tests predict college grades equally well for whites and members of minority ethnic groups (Cleary, 1968; Kendrick, 1967–68; Flaugher, 1970; Kendrick and Thomas, 1970). (What *grades* predict is a different question.) Even where differential predictions exist, the inaccuracies tend to *favor* minority youth and not to discriminate against them (Cleary, 1968; Temp, 1971). If anything, the results of research indicate that for blacks test scores are better predictors of college grades than are high school grades (McKelpin, 1965; Munday, 1965; Thomas and Stanley, 1969; Kendrick and Thomas, 1970).

Probably no single aspect of equality of educational opportunity has received as much attention as testing. In one sense the furor over test bias has served as a smoke screen obscuring the ethnic bias of the schools and of the larger society. Tests have, after all, paraded the problems of poor schooling for all to see. It is more comfortable and quite a bit easier to get rid of the thermometer that shows the fever than to cure the causes of the fever.

As we move into an egalitarian era, we need to explore ways of maximizing learning for a very diverse population of learners. Test development and use will need, like all other phases of education, to undergo drastic change. Tests may play a critical role in egalitarian higher education, but tests of the future will be much broader in scope and will be used to help the student and not to judge him. Tests directed toward comparison with others are irrelevant in egalitarian education, but tests used by students and teachers to diagnose individual learning strengths and weaknesses and to serve as guides for placement and counseling are among the strongest tools of individualized instruction.

Sex and College-Attendance Rates

Culture plays a strong role in shaping attitudes about appropriate sex roles. Correctly or incorrectly, many people have stereotyped notions about whether various ethnic subcultures are matriarchal or patriarchal, perceiving a strong role for women in the black culture and a weak role for them in Oriental and Spanish/Mexican cultures. Rates of college attendance seem to follow these perceptions. Oriental and Spanish/Mexican women are much less likely than men of their race to attend college, while black American women are a little more likely than their brothers to pursue education beyond high school. In 1968, according to the ACE national survey (Bayer and Boruch, 1969), 54 per cent of the black college freshmen were women—a substantially greater proportion than the college population of nonblacks, where 43 per cent were women. In fact, Knoell (1970) found that black women were not only more likely to attend college than black men, but, in four of the five cities studied, they were more likely to enter college than white women of similar ability.

Table 27 shows the percentages of males in each ethnic group who were attending college in the fall of 1969. In the CGP sample, for example, 77 per cent of the Orientals attending community colleges were male, while the remainder (23 per cent) were female. Although the figures differ because of sample differences and because the CGP sample represents two-year colleges whereas the SCOPE sample includes both two-year and four-year colleges and universities, the *patterns* for the two samples are quite similar.

While being female is apparently a barrier to college in some ethnic cultures, it is not in others. Oriental females are definitely

Table 27. COLLEGE-GOING MALES IN TWO SAMPLES

Ethnic Status	CGP	SCOPE
	Per Cent	*Per Cent*
Oriental	77	63
Spanish-American/Mexican	68	58
Caucasian	65	49
American Indian	59	54
Black American	46	50
Percentage of Males in Total Sample	63	49

Source: CGP, 1969; SCOPE 1969 data analysis by Tillery and Associates.

handicapped relative to Oriental males; only one fourth to one third of the Orientals in college are women. But since the college-attendance rates of Orientals are fairly high, Oriental women, handicapped as they are by sex, still have an educational advantage over Spanish American women, who are doubly handicapped by both race and sex. Other data from SCOPE indicate that approximately

44 per cent of the Oriental women entered college in 1969, compared with 37 per cent of the Spanish American/Mexican women.

Factors in Recruitment

A great deal of criticism has been leveled at secondary school counselors for their alleged failure to encourage minority youth to attend college. Few data are available on this important point, but what does exist does not support the validity of the criticism. Blacks who entered college in 1968 were more likely than nonblacks to attribute their college attendance to high school teachers and counselors. In the ACE survey (Bayer and Boruch, 1969), 43 per cent of the blacks but only 26 per cent of the nonblacks gave teachers or counselors credit for exerting a major influence in their decisions to attend particular colleges. Furthermore, this difference did not vary much with the type of college attended; 46 per cent of the blacks and 21 per cent of the nonblacks enrolled in predominantly white universities credited teachers and counselors as being major influences in their choices of college, whereas the corresponding ratios for two-year colleges were 46 per cent and 29 per cent. The most logical explanation for the relatively important role played by teachers and counselors in the college choices of black students is that black parents would be less likely to have information about colleges. But this seems not to be the explanation, since black students are also more likely than white students to say that parents played a major role in their choice of college (54 per cent for blacks to 48 per cent for nonblacks).

There is some evidence that college recruitment efforts were proving effective for blacks in 1968. Across all types of institutions —from two-year colleges to four-year universities—blacks were more likely than nonblacks to say that a major influence in their decision to attend the college was a graduate or a representative of the college (Bayer and Boruch, 1969). Although the influence of college recruiters was not ranked high by large numbers of blacks (17 per cent) or nonblacks (12 per cent), such influences still ranked fifth and sixth, respectively, out of a list of thirteen possible choices offered in the ACE questionnaire.

In general, black students tend to attribute their choice of college to other people, whereas nonblacks seem slightly more likely to base their decisions on characteristics of the college. For example, among the questionnaire alternatives attracting more than 15 per cent of the college freshmen, a larger percentage of blacks than non-blacks attributed major influence to parents or other relatives, teachers or counselors, or graduates or other college representatives. Nonblacks were slightly more likely than blacks to say that they were influenced by the academic reputation of the college or by low cost. In the interpretation of data collected from college students, one very important fact must be kept in mind: Blacks who are *in* college may attribute major influences to high school teachers and counseling services; but what about those who are *not* in college? Only longitudinal research can throw some much-needed light on that question.

Prognosis

Numerous factors are combining to increase the numbers of minority youth in college. But of greatest importance is probably the direct attack upon race as a barrier to higher education. Despite the gloomy prognostications of some (Astin, 1970; Egerton, 1970), the overall weight of the evidence seems to be that the gap between educational opportunities for majority and minority youth is narrowing. The Bureau of the Census reported that total college enrollment had increased 46 per cent from the fall of 1964 to the fall of 1968, while black enrollments had shown an 85 per cent increase. Furthermore, black enrollments increased 144 per cent in predominantly white institutions and only 30 per cent in black colleges (*Higher Education and National Affairs*, February 13, 1970). Other studies indicate similar acceleration in minority enrollments. In a survey by the National Association of State Universities and Land-Grant Colleges, over half of the institutions with available information about race showed a 50 per cent increase from 1968 to 1969 in the number of entering black freshmen (AAHE, 1970). A study of 129 four-year colleges in the Midwest reported a gross increase of 25 per cent in the number of minority freshmen enrolled in 1969 over the enrollments for 1968 (Midwest Committee for Higher Education Surveys, 1970). And a City University of New York study showed that the percentage of black and Puerto Rican undergraduate students in its system had increased from 13 per cent in 1967 to 22 per cent in 1970 (*New York Times,* December 23, 1970).

The picture does not look as encouraging for some of the other minority groups. The Governor's Committee on Public School Education in Texas (1968) found that the overall high school graduation rate in Texas is low—62 per cent; but it is 52 per cent for blacks and only 40 per cent for Mexican Americans. The Committee predicted that not until 1975 would the situation improve to the extent that half of the Mexican Americans in Texas would have completed high school.

Nationally the gap between the *median* education of nonwhites and whites started to narrow dramatically in the mid-1960s. In 1962, there was a gap of 3.1 years between the education levels of white and nonwhite males; by 1967, the median education of white males (who were over 18 and in the labor force) was 12.3, compared to 10.2 for nonwhite men—a difference of 1.9 years. For women the convergence has been even more rapid. In 1967, the median years of school completed by nonwhite women in the labor force was 11.5, compared with 12.4 for white women—a difference of only 0.9 years (Brimmer, 1969).

Despite recent gains, the actual proportion of minority youth in college remains pitifully small. Some researchers (Astin, 1970; Egerton, 1970) maintain that the efforts of white institutions to recruit minority youth have resulted merely in a redistribution of the existing pool of minority freshmen—that is, they have been encouraged to go to white colleges instead of to black colleges or to four-year institutions instead of two-year colleges. The large number of black youth now attending two-year colleges in their home cities seems to contradict that interpretation. Knoell (1970) found that half of all black college students in Fort Worth and San Francisco entered community colleges as freshmen and that black high school graduates were availing themselves of community college opportunities to a greater extent than were whites.

Much remains to be done before membership in an ethnic minority group ceases to be a barrier to equal educational opportunity. Research studies and individual recruiters still find able minority youth with talent and interest in higher education who are not planning to attend college (Rice, 1970). Knoell (1970) observes:

There are still some graduates with talent and interest who are being overlooked in the large cities, perhaps because the high schools from which they have graduated have sent so few to college in the past. Certainly the college recruiters might well concentrate on the schools—black and predominantly white—with low college-attendance rates, to discover the capable graduates who have yet to meet their first college recruiter. The talented in the schools which have traditionally sent their graduates to college are being re-re-cruited by college after college, to the point where they are confused and then bored by the abundance of offers. Recruitment may become necessary during the early years in high school or at the junior high school level, in order to encourage the would-be dropouts to complete their high school programs in anticipation of college [p. 180].

Almost anyone writing about the problems of assuring members of ethnic minorities equality of educational opportunity concludes the review of statistics by recommending that we start to correct the injustices at the earliest possible age, and the logic of that position cannot be faulted. But even if we eradicated the poor learning environments of minority youngsters tomorrow, the prospective candidates for higher education in the next decade are already in the first grade. For at least the next several decades, higher education will be held accountable for devising the methods that can assist in eradicating the educational disadvantages of minority youth born in a majority culture.

References

American Association for Higher Education. *College and University Bulletin,* May 1, 1970.

American Council on Education. *A Fact Book on Higher Education: Enrollment Data.* Washington, D.C.: ACE, first issue, 1970.

ASTIN, A. "Racial Considerations in Admissions." In D. Nichols and O. Mills, (eds.), *The Campus and the Racial Crisis.* Washington, D.C.: American Council on Education, 1970.

BAYER, A., AND R. BORUCH. *The Black Student in American Colleges.* ACE Research Reports, 4(2). Washington, D.C.: American Council on Education, 1969.

BRIMMER, A. F. "The Black Revolution and the Economic Future of Negroes in the United States." Commencement Address, Tennessee Agricultural and Industrial State University, June 8, 1969.

COLEMAN, J., et al. *Equality of Educational Opportunities.* Washington, D.C.: Government Printing Office, 1966.

CLEARY, T. A. "Test Bias: Prediction of Grades of Negro and White Students in Integrated Colleges." *Journal of Educational Measurement,* 1968, 5(2), 115–124.

EGERTON, J. "Inflated Body Count." *Change,* 1970, 2(4), 13–15.

FLAUGHER, R. *Testing Practices, Minority Groups, and Higher Education: A Review and Discussion of the Research.* Research Bulletin No. 70–41. Princeton: Educational Testing Service, 1970.

FROOMKIN, J. *Aspirations, Enrollments and Resources.* Planning Paper No. 69–1, Office of Planning and Evaluation, U.S. Office of Education. Washington, D.C.: Government Printing Office, 1969.

Governor's Committee on Public School Education in Texas. *The Challenge and the Chance.* Austin, August 31, 1968.

Higher Education and National Affairs. American Council on Education. February 13, 1970; December 4, 1970.

KATZ, I. "Experimental Studies of Negro-White Relationships." In L. Berkowitz, ed., *Advances in Experimental Psychology,* Vol. 5. New York: Academic Press, 1970.

KENDRICK, S. A. "The Coming Segregation of Our Selective Colleges." *College Board Review,* 1967–68, 66, 6–12.

——————. "Extending Educational Opportunity—Problems of Recruitment, Admissions, High Risk Students." *Liberal Education,* 1969, 15(1), 12–17.

——————, AND C. L. THOMAS. "Transition from School to College." *Review of Educational Research,* 1970, 40(1), 151–179.

KNOELL, D. M. *People Who Need College.* Washington, D.C.: American Association of Junior Colleges, 1970.

Midwest Committee for Higher Education Surveys. *Admissions of Minority Students in Midwestern Colleges.* Report M-1. Evanston, Illinois: College Entrance Examination Board, 1970.

MC KELPIN, J. P. "Some Implications of the Intellectual Characteristics of Freshmen Entering a Liberal Arts College." *Journal of Educational Measurement*, 1965, 2, 161–166.

MUNDAY, L. "Predicting Grades in Predominantly Negro Colleges." *Journal of Educational Measurement*, 1965, 2, 157–160.

RICE, L. D. "A Larger Talent Pool." In D. Nichols and O. Mills, eds., *The Campus and the Racial Crisis*. Washington, D.C.: American Council on Education, 1970.

RIESSMAN, F. *The Culturally Deprived Child*. New York: Harper & Row, 1962.

SOWELL, T. "Colleges Are Skipping Over Competent Blacks to Admit 'Authentic' Ghetto Types." *New York Times Magazine*, December 13, 1970.

TEMP, G. *Test Bias: Validity of the SAT for Blacks and Whites in Thirteen Integrated Institutions*. College Entrance Examination Board Research and Development Reports, RDR-7-71, No. 6. Princeton: Educational Testing Service, January 1971.

THOMAS, C. L., AND J. C. STANLEY. "Effectiveness of High School Grades for Predicting College Grades of Black Students: A Review and Discussion." *Journal of Educational Measurement*, 1969, 6(4), 203–215.

TILLERY, D., AND ASSOCIATES. SCOPE data, 1969. Berkeley: Center for Research and Development in Higher Education, University of California. Unpublished.

WOMEN AS
NEW STUDENTS

9

The sex barrier to higher education has not received as much attention as the barrier imposed by ethnic minority status, but numerically women constitute by far the largest reservoir of youthful talent not presently continuing education beyond high school. In the fall of 1969, 52 per cent of the men between the ages of 20 and 24 had completed some college, compared with 42 per cent of the women. The rate of college attendance is increasing more rapidly now for women than for men, but at the present time the national ratio of men to women in college is an unbalanced 59 to 41 (ACE *Fact Book*, 1970).

According to U.S. Department of Labor figures (1968), the ratios of first-time college enrollees to high school graduates for the past seventeen years are these: In 1950, 56 per cent of the males and 31 per cent of the females graduating from high school entered college; in 1960, the percentages had increased to 60 per cent of the males and 40 per cent of the females; by 1967 approximately 71 per cent of the males and 54 per cent of the females were entering college. Whereas almost three fourths of the male high school graduates enter college today, the college-attendance rate for women

133

climbed over 50 per cent as recently as 1966—a mark attained by men more than twenty years ago.

In the past, more women than men have graduated from high school. In 1960, for example, 67 girls out of a hundred who reached 17 years of age completed high school, compared with 64 boys per hundred. But the high school graduation gap has been steadily narrowing; in 1967, high school graduating classes were composed of 50.3 per cent women and 49.7 per cent men. Thus, the pool of potential college applicants is now equally distributed by sex.

The male-female ratio differs considerably depending upon the type of institution. The largest proportion of women are attending state colleges, which have a history of emphasis upon the training of elementary and secondary school teachers. Even in these institutions, however, male students predominate. Enrollment ratios are 53 per cent male and 47 per cent female (Dunham, 1969); at the other end of the continuum stand the private universities, where the ratio is 69 men to 31 women (Simon and Grant, 1969).

Most colleges can expect the proportion of women in their student bodies to increase rapidly during the decade of the 1970s for several reasons: (1) Education is becoming increasingly important to women as more and more women enter the labor market. The U.S. Department of Labor Women's Bureau has reported that in 1970 almost half of all women between the ages of 18 and 65 were in the labor force, and more than half of these workers were married women. (2) The reservoir of academically qualified women not now going to college is large. Knoell (1970) concluded that, of all potential college students, able white women constitute the group most neglected by college recruitment personnel. In one city included in her study of black and white youth she found that the *lowest* rate of college attendance for young people with I.Q.s above 105 occurred among white women. (3) The new attention directed to obtaining equality of opportunity for women is part of the broader egalitarian movement. If women were to enter institutions of higher education in the same proportion as men, about one and a half million new students would enter our colleges.

For all these reasons, it is probably safe to predict that within the next five years universities will move away from their traditional ratios of six or seven men to every three or four women. The former teachers' colleges will attract more men as they continue their move toward multipurpose institutions. And community colleges will move away from their heavily male enrollments as women from the lower socioeconomic and ability levels begin to enter institutions of higher education.

What are the characteristics of this group of New Students to higher education?

Academic Ability

Unlike other groups of New Students, women as a group are well qualified by traditional standards to undertake college work. Traditional tests of academic aptitude usually show a slight female superiority in verbal abilities, whereas men outscore women on quantitative measures. When verbal and quantitative measures are combined, as they usually are in the admissions process, men have slightly better total test scores than women. On the other hand, when grades are used as the measure of academic accomplishment, women receive markedly higher grade-point averages than men. To give a very rough example of relationships, in the form of the percentages that are used throughout this book, 49 per cent of the college-bound males and 43 per cent of the females scored above the mean score of a quarter million young people on the composite test score of the American College Tests; 51 per cent of the men and 68 per cent of the women had high school grade-point averages of 2.5 ($C+$) or better (Hoyt and Munday, 1968).

There is no lack of data on the abilities of men and women as they are measured by tests. Long before women's rights movements began demanding national attention, test norms were being published separately for males and females, simply because they were easily identifiable groups that showed significant differences in performance. And yet the differences between test scores of males and females are not nearly as great as those between other groups in which we are now interested—upper and lower socioeconomic groups or majority and minority ethnic groups, for instance. The practice of sex-differentiated test norms probably started when abilities were assumed innate, but the case for innate differences in the academic ability of men and women is no easier to make than that for innate differences between blacks and whites. In all probability, girls learn verbal abilities and boys learn quantitative and mechanical abilities from their cultural surroundings. The Project TALENT staff (Flanagan et al., 1964), after a thorough study of the cognitive abilities of young people, concluded that "When very large differences occur between scores of boys and girls, they almost always reflect great differences between the sexes in amount of interest" (p. 32).

Data from the admissions testing program of the American College Testing Program reflect typical sex differences on subject-matter tests. Table 28 shows the mean scores for a group of college-bound high school seniors in 1966–67. These data show a near draw on the test scores of men and women. Women score higher in English, men score higher in mathematics and science; there is virtually no difference in social studies. When the four scores are averaged to give a composite score, the total difference between the mean total test scores of men and women is very small indeed.

Table 28. MEAN ACT SCORES OF COLLEGE-BOUND STUDENTS (1966–67)

Test	Male	Female	Difference
English	17.8	20.0	−2.2
Mathematics	20.1	17.8	2.3
Social Studies	20.1	19.9	0.2
Natural Sciences	21.4	19.4	2.0
Composite	20.0	19.4	0.6

Source: Hoyt and Munday, 1968.

College-bound students, as a group, score higher on tests of academic aptitude than do students from the broader population of high school seniors, but the male-female patterns of test scores remain similar. Table 29 shows the mean scores on the Scholastic Aptitude Test (SAT) for a national sample representative of all secondary school seniors compared with students who planned to enter college in 1969–70. On the SAT, there is almost no difference in the average scores of males and females on the verbal portion, but men score considerably higher on the mathematical section.

The single best predictor of college performance is the high school record. And there can be no equivocation about the superior academic achievement of women when measured by the traditional grading system. Studies going back as far as 1929 show better grades for females from elementary school through college (Anastasi, 1958). The grades of women high school students are quite significantly above those of men. For 1960 Project TALENT seniors, 51 per cent of the girls and 39 per cent of the boys reported high school averages of "mostly *A*'s and *B*'s" or above. The 1969 SCOPE data contained the same message; 60 per cent of the senior girls and 44 per cent of the boys reported grades that were "mostly *B*'s" or above. Men are much more likely than women to enter college with border-

Table 29. MEAN SCORES FOR ALL HIGH SCHOOL SENIORS AND FOR COLLEGE-BOUND SENIORS (1969–70)

	Males	Females
SAT Verbal		
High School Seniors	390	393
College-Bound Seniors	457	458
SAT Mathematical		
High School Seniors	422	382
College-Bound Seniors	506	461

Source: *College Board Score Reports,* 1970.

line grades of *C*+ or lower: 35 per cent for men to 19 per cent for women (ACE, 1970b). At the college level, the story is the same. In the spring of 1970, for example, 46 per cent of the freshmen women at the University of California at Berkeley made first-semester grade averages of *B* or better, compared with 39 per cent of the men. For seniors, the figures were almost identical; 45 per cent of the senior women and 38 per cent of the senior men had spring semester averages of *B* or above.

Girls not only have better grade-point averages, but they are even likely—at least in high school—to win the top grades in the traditionally masculine fields of mathematics and science. At the high school level, girls are more likely than boys to make A's and B's in the four major subject-matter areas of English (46 per cent of the males, 73 per cent of the females), mathematics (37 per cent males, 44 per cent females), social sciences (53 per cent males, 66 per cent females), and natural sciences (40 per cent males and 52 per cent females). Reference to Table 28, which reports data for this same sample of students, shows that boys knew more science and mathematics when tests were used as the measure; girls knew more when grades served as the criterion. Is the explanation simply that boys are better test-takers and girls are better grade-getters? Perhaps. But perhaps also—because science and mathematics, especially at the junior and senior levels, are likely to be electives—girls who are quite good at science elect science, whereas average and below-average boys may choose to study mathematics and science. Adults in the society—parents, teachers, and counselors—undoubtedly influence these choices. A girl may have to be quite insistent if she wishes to enter scientific fields of study, and a boy who prefers English may have to resist being pushed toward more "masculine" interests.

The concentration of high-achieving students in the student body varies, of course, with the type of institution. Sex differences in academic achievement tend to be greatest in the less selective institutions, narrowing somewhat as the colleges become more selective. The explanation for the large male-female grade differences in non-selective colleges lies in the fact that boys with poor academic records enter open-door colleges, whereas girls with poor records do not enter college at all; some go to work and some enter beauty schools or business colleges. Selective institutions tend to select both men and women from the pool of high-performance students, thus narrowing the differences in academic achievement.

Academic Motivation

The synthesis of research about test scores and grades as indicators of academic ability leads to the conclusion, badly put, that women are slightly behind men on test scores but are significantly ahead on grades. What accounts for the apparent success of women in academic activities? I say "apparent success" because grades are only one measure of academic accomplishment, and not an especially satisfactory one at that (Warren, 1971). Nevertheless, grades are the coin of the realm; and teachers, parents, students, and employers agree that grades shall signify the level of academic accomplishment. Most students want good grades and try to attain them; yet girls are better at getting grades than boys are, and this is true at both high school and college levels.

The many explanations offered include the frequent observations that girls tend to be more conscientious, conforming, and docile in the classroom; that women manipulate their (primarily male) instructors to obtain higher grades (Singer, 1964); and that traits such as neatness, punctuality, and regular attendance contribute to the higher grades of women (Caldwell and Hartnett, 1967). The theories of the female college student's using her wiles on the male professor fail to explain the superior grades of elementary and secondary school girls; however, the theories based on conscientiousness and docility do have some basis in research. More girls than boys admit to being conscientious about school work. Among Project TALENT high school seniors, 39 per cent of the girls but only 22 per cent of the boys maintained that they "almost always" kept up to date on school assignments (Flanagan et al., 1964). Among four-year-college freshmen responding to the College Student Questionnaires (CSQ, 1966) women were more likely than men to say that they had studied harder than their high school classmates (62 per cent for women to 52 per cent for men), that their fellow students perceived them as hard workers (76 per cent to 63 per cent), and that their teachers thought of them as hard workers (64 per cent to 44 per cent). Interestingly enough, there is only a 10 per cent difference between males and females when they are commenting on how hard they think they work; but there is a 20 per cent difference when they are asked to judge teachers' ratings of their industry. Men seem to feel that their teachers underestimate their efforts— which may account in part for boys' feelings of dissatisfaction with their grades; 56 per cent of the CSQ freshmen men and 37 per cent of the women said that their high school grades underrepresented their ability. Do boys simply have a more difficult time convincing teachers that they are working hard? Maybe, but it also appears that girls spend more actual hours on homework than boys do. Among high school seniors, girls were almost twice as likely as boys (31 per cent to 16 per cent) to spend more than two hours a day on homework (Tillery et al., 1966). The percentages of students devoting long hours to study increased dramatically when the same question was put to the more selective sample of college freshmen, but the difference between the sexes still heavily favored the longer study hours of women; 74 per cent of the women and 59 per cent of the men said that as high school seniors they had studied more than two hours a day (CSQ, 1966). If girls spend more time studying lessons that are presumably worthwhile, it seems quite reasonable that they should learn more and that grades should reflect their academic accomplishment.

Why girls should strive for academic achievement is not an easy question to answer, apart from the observation that society considers it more acceptable for a female to be conscientious than for a male—at least in the early years of life. Actually, grades as such appear to be less important to girls than to boys in determining their futures. Neither the continuation of their education nor the jobs attained after graduation are as closely linked to academic prowess for girls as for boys. Furthermore, the folklore would have us believe that there is a negative relationship between school achievement and dating and marriage.

How do girls view grades? The great majority of high school seniors think grades are either "very important" or "one of the most important things in my life." Thirteen per cent of the boys and 12 per cent of the girls gave the latter answer, and 66 per cent of the boys and 71 per cent of the girls gave one of these two responses. Even larger numbers of students (80 percent of the girls and 74 per cent of the boys), however, think that learning as much as possible in school should rank equally high in their priorities (Tillery et al., 1966). Among college freshmen responding to the College Student Questionnaires (CSQ, 1966) 33 per cent of the women and 28 per cent of the men attached a "great deal" of importance to grades. The importance of school work to both sexes is revealed by the finding that in the CSQ sample more students wanted to be remembered as a brilliant student in their high school (46 per cent for both sexes) than as an outstanding athlete, as a leader in activities, or as most popular. It is hard to make a case that girls are much more interested in grades than boys are.

The differences between the sexes are a little greater, but not startlingly so, when some of the common purposes of education are considered. Most college-bound students, a little over half of each sex, indicate that their major goal in attending college is to secure vocational training; but women are more likely than men (38 per cent to 29 per cent) to say that the development of the mind and intellectual abilities is an important goal (ACT, 1966). Among the high school seniors in the American College Testing Program, a higher percentage of women than men (47 per cent to 37 per cent) felt that "intellectual atmosphere" should be a major factor in choosing a college, and 67 per cent of the women and 57 per cent of the men said they were looking for a college with high scholastic standards. Figures are similar for the 10,000 high school graduates studied by Trent and Medsker (1968). Women who entered college were a little more likely than men (52 per cent to 44 per cent) to be interested in the more general purposes of education (gaining of knowledge, understanding of world problems, and appreciation of ideas). But the differences seem related more to the relatively high achievement level of women who enter college than to sex. The SCOPE study found very small sex differences, in the unselected high school senior population, in the responses of males and females to a list of fifteen factors influencing their choice of college. Women were slightly more interested in teaching reputation and the friendliness of the college environment; men were more interested in a good athletic program, and there was not even a 5 per cent difference on the remaining twelve items (Tillery et al., 1966).

In an intensive study of the intellectual values of college students, Heist and Yonge (1968) found statistically significant differences between the sexes on the scales of the Omnibus Personality Inventory (OPI). Of the four OPI scales that contribute most heavily to "the potential for behaving intellectually," women scored higher on fondness for working with ideas and abstractions in a variety of areas such as literature, art, and philosophy (Thinking Introversion) and on esthetic appreciations (Estheticism); men scored higher on interest in theoretical problems and the use of the scientific method in thinking (Theoretical Orientation); and there was no difference between the sexes in flexibility and tolerance for ambiguities and uncertainties (Complexity).

A review of the major measures of academic interest and ability leaves little room for argument with the conclusion that there are no important differences between men and women in their potentials for academic accomplishment. Furthermore, the data indicate that women as a group are every bit as interested in the goals and activities of higher education as men are. There is no evidence that women are less interested in ideas or less able to work constructively with them. On measures of academic ability, academic accomplishment, and academic interests and motivations, women constitute an impressive group of New Students to higher education.

Socioeconomic Status

Family socioeconomic status is an important determinant of who goes where to college. We know, from many studies, that encouragement from parents bears a high relationship to college attendance. In our society, parents seem to feel that it is more important for a son to go to college than for a daughter. Forty-nine per cent of the SCOPE senior boys stated that their mothers "definitely desired" college for them, whereas only 37 per cent of the girls reported as much parental enthusiasm for continued education. Census Bureau interviewers found, however, that the higher the educational level of the parents, the less they were likely to distinguish between the educational needs of sons and daughters. For example, 73 per cent of the mothers with a grade school education wanted college for their sons, but only 60 per cent expressed the same desire for their daughters. Among mothers who had attended college, there was virtually no difference in the education desired for boys and girls; 98 per cent wanted sons to go to college and 97 per cent wanted college for their daughters (Froomkin, 1970).

Because low family socioeconomic status is still a barrier to college for women, college women as a group tend to come from a slightly higher socioeconomic status (SES) than men. For example, in the nationwide ACE sample of college freshmen 46 per cent of the women and 41 per cent of the men came from homes where fathers had attended college; if an occupational index is used, 28 per cent of the men and 24 per cent of the women are from blue-collar homes (Creager et al., 1969).

Despite the fact that college women come from higher-SES homes than do college men, women are a little more likely than men to list financing their education as a "major concern" (Creager et al., 1969), and they are also somewhat more likely than men to select "expense" as the most probable obstacle to future college attendance (Tillery et al., 1966). A comprehensive study of the college-attendance rates of New York state youth (New York State Education Department, 1969) reported that the lack of money does operate as a barrier to educational opportunities for women. Significantly more women than men changed their college plans because of financial limitations. Even after they enter low-cost public community colleges, women are more likely than men to be troubled by lack of money. Forty per cent of the women and 33 per cent of the men say that they would like the college to help them find a job, and 32 per cent of the women and 26 per cent of the men say that they need financial aid (CGP, 1970).

Much female concern with financing a college education is related to the probable source of funds. SCOPE data collected from high school seniors who were planning or hoping to enter some institution of postsecondary education reveal that girls intend to rely somewhat more heavily on financial support from their parents while boys will draw more on earnings from past jobs or from summer or part-time jobs during college. When asked the source from which they expected to receive at least half of their college expenses, 54 per cent of the girls and 45 per cent of the boys mentioned parents. The other sources mentioned were loans (28 per cent of the males, 24 per cent of the females), their own savings (27 per cent of the males, 20 per cent of the females), summer or college jobs (23 per cent of the males, 18 per cent of the females), and scholarships (11 per cent of the males, 8 per cent of the females). The differences between the sexes in the probable sources of funds are not as large as one might expect, given the fact that three influences all push in the direction of female dependence and male independence in financing a college education: (1) as a group, college-attending girls come from homes a little better able to help with college expenses than boys do; (2) jobs, either during the high school or college years, are easier for boys to obtain; (3) the norms of society are more permissive regarding female financial dependence.

These mores of society are reflected in data from the New York study of college attendance (New York State Education Department, 1969), which found that more boys than girls were willing to borrow for their education (56 per cent to 44 per cent) and to work part time (65 per cent to 61 per cent). A very high proportion of both men and women were planning to seek summer employment (86 per cent and 82 per cent).

A synthesis of the data on socioeconomic status presented in this chapter and in Chapter 1 leads to the conclusion that females as such have one strike against them when the probability of a college education is considered; a female from a low socioeconomic background has two strikes against her, and, if she is also not a very good student, she is quite likely to strike out. Ethnic status, as has been noted, is not a consistent handicap; it depends upon the role of the female in the culture.

Educational Aspirations

Many people, including educators, attribute the minority status of women in college to low educational aspirations, pointing out that many high school girls prefer marriage to college. However, fewer than three out of one hundred high school senior girls plan to get married upon graduation from high school, and seventy out of one hundred expect to go to college sometime (Tillery et al., 1966). Most high school graduates today do aspire to college. It is not primarily at the point of college entrance that the male-female discrepancies in educational aspirations occur; rather, it is in the amount of higher education they hope eventually to obtain. Table 30 shows the educational aspirations of high school seniors in the 1969 SCOPE sample.

The dividing line between the aspirations of boys and girls falls between the junior college and the four-year-college degree. Just over half the women will be content with two years of college or less, whereas slightly over half of the men aspire to four years of college or more. Among freshmen enrolled in college in the fall of 1969, 57 per cent of the men and 43 per cent of the women planned to go beyond the bachelor's degree (Creager et al., 1969).

Table 30.   EDUCATIONAL ASPIRATIONS OF HIGH SCHOOL SENIORS
SPRING 1969

Aspiration	Male	Female	Total
	Per Cent	*Per Cent*	*Per Cent*
Leave school or graduate from high school	17	21	19
Junior college, business or vocational school	24	31	28
Graduate from a four-year institution	34	35	34
Postgraduate work	20	10	14
No response	5	4	4

Source: Tillery and Associates, 1969.

Self-Concept

Much of the reason for the lower educational aspirations of women is to be found in the attitudes of society. Girls receive less encouragement from their parents and from society at large to achieve at high levels. A characteristic that women have in common with other groups of people who have not been a part of the dominant culture is the problem of diminished self-concept. Much as members of ethnic minorities have been encouraged to set their aspirations "realistically" for jobs that would be "open" to them, women have been encouraged to think about elementary school teaching rather than college teaching, about typing instead of business management, and about becoming nurses rather than doctors. These constant reminders of a secondary role in society take a toll, and the results are clearly evident in the research.

Women are significantly less likely than men to believe, as high school seniors, that they "definitely have the ability" to do college work. Despite their better high school grades, which should represent an independent measure of success to them, only 26 per cent of the women compared with 35 per cent of the men in the

SCOPE sample expressed a high level of confidence in their academic ability (Tillery et al., 1966). Furthermore, there appears to be some personal cost involved in the surface adjustment of girls to the classroom. Over one third of the high school girls said that they often feel nervous, tense, or shy in class; less than one fourth of the boys admitted to these feelings of insecurity. The problem can be said to have reached serious proportions for women in the lowest third of the class academically, with 44 per cent stating that they are frequently uncomfortable in class (SCOPE data, 1966). These sex differences in anxiety levels occur very early in the child's schooling. In a study of second-grade children Katz (1968) reported higher anxiety scores for girls than for boys among white pupils, but not for blacks. There is some evidence that black women do not play the same secondary role in education relative to males that white women do (see Chapter 8).

It is hard to say why classroom anxiety is so prevalent among young women. Actually, according to 1966 SCOPE data, male high school seniors are more likely than females to feel that the teachers go too fast (21 per cent for boys and 15 per cent for girls) and that there is too much stress on grades (36 per cent for boys and 28 per cent for girls). One would think that both of these situations might be anxiety-provoking. Apparently, it is not the academic tasks themselves that account for feelings of tension or shyness among young women.

Chapter 2 sets forth the thesis that a major characteristic of our classrooms from first grade through graduate school is their hotly competitive nature. And, the data reveal, women do not enjoy competition as much as men do; 26 per cent of the women entering college, but only 13 per cent of the men, confessed to disliking competitive situations (CSQ, 1966). In particular, women have been taught not to enjoy competing with men. But school is a competitive situation, and in this competition girls seem threatened by winning. Encouraged to know the answers in school but discouraged from proving it, many adolescent girls may develop approach-avoidance conflicts.

Whereas the interests of men are directed toward attaining status in a competitive world, the interests of college women conform to the expected feminine passive or nurturant roles. Larger percentages of women than men express interest in helping people in difficulty, raising a family, creating art, developing a philosophy of life, and influencing social values. Men, by contrast, express more competitive drive by valuing achievements such as becoming authorities in their fields, obtaining recognition from peers, becoming administratively responsible, and attaining financial and business success (Creager et al., 1969). In some respects, college women of the past have been protected from competitive situations by virtue of enrolling in women's fields. Nurses, for instance, do not compete with doctors either in study or in career performance.

Women's Roles

Women's roles in society are changing now—much more rapidly than those of men. The rate of growth of women in the labor market is increasing five times as rapidly for women as for men. Ninety per cent of all women work at some time during their lives, and the typical girl graduating from high school today may expect to work outside the home for twenty-five years of her life. College women are well aware of the changing sex roles, and some recent data show the changes in attitudes to be extremely rapid. Not many colleges collect information about student attitudes year after year, but were they to do so, they would find some very interesting trends. One women's college has administered the College Student Questionnaires (CSQ) to the entering freshman class each year since 1964 (College Research Center, 1971). The most dramatic changes to take place over the years occurred in student perceptions about women's roles. One question asked what the respondent would like to be doing fifteen years hence. Sixty-five per cent of the 1964 class said they would like to be a housewife with one or more children. Over the years, there was a steady decline in the percentage choosing this life style—until, in 1970, only 31 per cent preferred the traditional female role. From 1964 to 1970, the percentages subscribing to a future as housewife and mother were as follows: 65, 61, 60, 53, 52, 46, 31. Two other alternatives increased in popularity: the percentage wanting to be a married career woman with children doubled, going from 20 per cent in 1964 to 40 per cent in 1970. And the percentage that were uncertain increased from 13 to 22 per cent, probably reflecting the strain that extremely rapid social change places on individuals. When asked to express their opinions about the role of adult women in American society, 19 per cent of the 1964 class and only 7 per cent of the 1970 class felt that the activities of women should be confined to home and family. Most dramatic of all, perhaps, were the responses to a question concerning career choice. In 1964, 57 per cent elected a career that would center around home and family; by 1970 the figure had dropped to less than half, 22 per cent. The slack was taken up by increases in almost any career area, but especially "academic life" and "professional life." Notice that the size of all of these percentages reflects a conservative student body. These are not "women's lib types." In 1965, for example, when 49 per cent of the women at the women's college where these studies were conducted were looking forward to a life centering on home and family, only 26 per cent of the women in the national sample were. The career aspirations of college women are rising; the evidence suggests that sex roles are changing very rapidly for young women today. Colleges ignore these trends to the peril of educating young people for adult roles in society.

Since the present social revolution affects women's roles more than men's, it is not surprising that college women experience more difficulty than men in knowing who they are and what they wish to become. When college students were asked to indicate their greatest problem in college, the only problem to show a significant difference between men and women was that of achieving a sense of identity. The search for identity was the most common problem for college women, with one third of them engaged in the quest. Achieving identity was the major problem for one fourth of the men (CSQ, 1968). The majority (51 per cent) of college women feel that today's woman should divide her time between a home, a job, and children. To juggle the often conflicting roles of wife, mother, and career woman is no small challenge.

Discrimination

When compared with the problems of racial discrimination in the society or with job discrimination against women, the cases of out-and-out discrimination against the admission of undergraduate women to college seem pale. Many educators flatly deny its existence. But even a moment's thought to how a selective university maintains a 65–35 sex ratio while accepting only one in four applicants should give rise to some questions. If the pool of highly qualified women is as large as the pool of highly qualified men— which it is—how does the 65–35 ratio maintain itself? Discrimination against women for admission to college is surprisingly easy to document in public as well as in private institutions. Table 31 shows one example of sex discrimination at the undergraduate level. These data were openly presented by the college in a handbook used for the guidance of high school seniors and their counselors. (Original data were given in numbers, not percentages, thus obscuring the operation of discriminatory practices for the average reader.)

The better grade-getting ability of girls seems more than adequately compensated for by the acceptance of 87 per cent of the male applicants from the top fifth of their high school class, compared to only 66 per cent of the women. If women score very high on the verbal portion of the SAT (over 700, which is the score of the top 1 per cent of high school graduates), their chances of obtaining admission to the college illustrated in Table 31 are as good as men's chances. But the closer a woman gets to being average, the more severe the discrimination becomes. The only admissions criterion at this college that does not show marked sex discrimination is mathematics test scores, but men are twice as likely as women to make very high SAT-M scores (11 per cent of the high school senior males and 5 per cent of the females score above 600). Women applicants to this college must be as good as males in mathematics and better than men in high school record and verbal aptitude in order to gain admission.

Generally speaking, very able women are not as likely to experience discrimination as are their average or below-average sisters—at least not until they reach a level of selectivity where they too have substantial competition, as in Ph.D. candidacy, for example. A group of investigators at the University of Wisconsin (*Transaction*, 1971) verified the existence of discrimination against lower-ability women by sending bogus applications to 240 colleges. They found that their invented applicant with high grades was as likely to be accepted as a male applicant with equally good grades. But male applicants with low ability were decidedly more likely to be accepted than females with the same low credentials.

Table 31. RATES OF ACCEPTANCE OF APPLICANTS TO A PRESTIGE
FOUR-YEAR LIBERAL-ARTS COLLEGE

| | Percentage of Applicants Accepted[a] | |
Criteria	Male	Female
	Per Cent	*Per Cent*
High school class rank		
Top fifth	87	66
Second fifth	44	14
Third fifth and below	22	20
SAT scores—verbal		
700–800	90	90
600–699	85	70
500–599	60	30
Below 500	22	16
SAT scores—mathematical		
700–800	89	87
600–699	79	71
500–599	44	39
Below 500	11	17

SOURCE: Computed from data given in *The College Handbook,* 1969.

[a] Applications for admission were received from 711 males and 601 females. Overall rates of acceptance were 72 per cent for males and 60 per cent for females.

Although it is hard to excuse discrimination on the part of educational institutions on the basis of race or sex or any other personal characteristic, public institutions have had to be considerably more circumspect about discriminatory practices than private institutions. But overt discrimination against women in higher education exists in public as well as in private institutions of higher education. Table 32 shows the percentage of male and female applicants accepted by a public state university based upon rank in high school graduating class. No other data were given.

On the face of it, it is difficult to understand why a respected public university should accept 83 per cent of the men and only 52 per cent of the women ranking in the second tenth of their class. This institution states that eligibility for admission is "determined by ability to meet minimums in two of the following three criteria: high school average, rank in class, test scores." Since on two out of three of the criteria—rank in class and grades—women are likely to

Table 32. Applicants Accepted by a State University in 1968

| Class Rank | Percentage of Applicants Accepted[a] | |
	Male	Female
	Per Cent	*Per Cent*
Top tenth	98	92
Second tenth	83	52
Third tenth	43	21
Fourth tenth	32	22
Fifth tenth	23	31
Lower half	41	25

Source: Computed from data given in *The College Handbook,* 1969.

[a] Total number of applicants was 1,835 men and 1,921 women.

meet minimum standards more readily than men, it would appear that this institution should actually have more women than men in its freshman class. Discrimination on this public campus seems particularly hard to defend, since the institution boasts a "wholly new campus," which should remove the dormitory-space problem, and advertises a curriculum that should have as much appeal for women as for men. The university has three colleges—a college of liberal arts, a four-year school of nursing, and a school of business. Despite the easy documentation of examples of discrimination by both private and public institutions of higher learning, the data regarding women's own feelings of discrimination are not quite so clear. Women, it seems, are somewhat more likely than men to be willing to face rejection by the college of their choice. Sixty-seven per cent of the women and 61 per cent of the men in the SCOPE sample (1969) maintained that, if they were to apply to a college, they would choose one they really wanted to attend even if their chances of getting in were uncertain. On the other hand, there is no evidence that women feel they will not be able to go to the college of their choice; as high school seniors, 39 per cent of the men and 38 per cent of the women thought they would actually enter the college of their choice in the fall. Perhaps, though, the more telling figures lie in the number of women who said as high school seniors that they planned to go to college, but who failed to enter college in the fall following their graduation. For women, the percentage of students falling in this category was 21 per cent; for men it was 18 per cent (Tillery et al., 1969). While the difference between these figures is very slight, it is statistically significant beyond the 0.01 level. We need not assume that these women failed to enter college because of discrimination on the part of the colleges. It is probable that society's little discouragements added together contributed to the disappointment of these women. Tight budgets, illness at home, marriage, and a host of other factors are more likely to deter women from college entrance than they are to discourage men.

In conclusion, it is a near certainty that the group of New Students to higher education will contain more women than men. All of the present trends—concern about the population explosion, drastic reductions in the amount of time devoted to cooking and care of the home, and an increasingly egalitarian public—are pushing in the direction of certifying the prediction. Colleges will face few special problems with instructional programs in accommodating the needs of women in higher education, but policies and practices in admissions, financial aids, career and academic advising, job placement, and housing regulations are due for change if all young people are to be assured equality of opportunity.

References

American College Testing Program (ACT). *College Student Profiles*. Iowa City: ACT, 1966.

American Council on Education. *A Fact Book on Higher Education: Enrollment Data*. First issue. Washington, D.C.: ACE, 1970. a

American Council on Education. *National Norms for Entering College Freshmen—Fall 1970*. ACE Research Report No. 6. Washington, D.C.: Office of Research, ACE, 1970. b

ANASTASI, A. *Differential Psychology*. New York: Macmillan, 1958.

CALDWELL, E., AND R. HARTNETT. "Sex Bias in College Grading?" *Journal of Educational Measurement*, 1967, *4*(3), 129–132.

College Board Score Reports. Preliminary SAT and Achievement Tests. Prepared for College Entrance Examination Board. Princeton: Educational Testing Service, 1970.

College Entrance Examination Board. *The College Handbook*. New York: CEEB, 1969.

College Research Center. *Reports to Member Colleges*. Princeton: Educational Testing Service, 1971.

College Student Questionnaires (CSQ). Part I: *Comparative Data*. Princeton: Educational Testing Service, 1966.

————. Part II: *Comparative Data*. Princeton: Educational Testing Service, 1968.

Comparative Guidance and Placement Program (CGP). *Program Summary Statistics, 1969–70*. Prepared for College Entrance Examination Board. Princeton: Educational Testing Service, 1970.

CREAGER, J. A., ASTIN, A. W., BORUCH, R. F., BAYER, A. E., AND DREW, D. E. *National Norms for Entering College Freshmen—Fall 1969*. ACE Research Reports, *4*(7). Washington, D.C.: American Council on Education, 1969.

DUNHAM, E. A. *Colleges of the Forgotten Americans*. New York: McGraw-Hill, 1969.

FLANAGAN, J. C., AND ASSOCIATES. *Project TALENT: The American High School Student*. Pittsburgh: Project TALENT, University of Pittsburgh, 1964.

FROOMKIN, J. *Aspirations, Enrollments, and Resources*. Prepared for U.S. Office of Education. Washington, D.C.: Government Printing Office, 1970.

HEIST, P., AND G. YONGE. *Omnibus Personality Inventory Manual, Form F.* New York: The Psychological Corporation, 1968.

HOYT, D., AND L. MUNDAY. *Your College Freshmen.* Iowa City: American College Testing Program, 1968.

KATZ, I. "Academic Motivation and Equal Educational Opportunity." *Harvard Educational Review,* 1968, *38*(1), 57–65.

KNOELL, DOROTHY M. *People Who Need College.* Washington, D.C.: American Association of Junior Colleges, 1970.

New York State Education Department. *A Longitudinal Study of the Barriers Affecting the Pursuit of Higher Education by New York State High School Seniors.* Albany, N.Y.: Office of Planning in Higher Education, University of the State of New York, 1969.

SIMON, K., AND V. GRANT. *Digest of Educational Statistics.* Prepared for U.S. Office of Education. Washington, D.C.: Government Printing Office, 1969.

SINGER, J. E. "The Use of Manipulative Strategies: Machiavellianism and Attractiveness." *Sociometry,* 1964, *27,* 128–150.

TILLERY, D., D. DONOVAN, AND B. SHERMAN. *SCOPE: Four-State Profile, Grade 12, 1966.* Prepared for College Entrance Examination Board. Berkeley: Center for Research and Development in Higher Education, University of California, 1966.

————. Unpublished 1969 SCOPE data. Center for Research and Development in Higher Education, University of California, Berkeley.

Transaction. "Women in College." January 1971, *8*(3).

TRENT, J. W., AND L. L. MEDSKER. *Beyond High School: A Psychological Study of 10,000 High School Graduates.* San Francisco: Jossey-Bass, 1968.

United States Department of Labor, Women's Bureau. *Trends in Educational Attainment of Women.* Washington, D.C.: Government Printing Office, 1968.

WARREN, J. R. "Current Grading Practices." *College and University Bulletin.* Research Report No. 3. Washington, D.C.: American Association for Higher Education, 1971.

NEW EDUCATION FOR NEW STUDENTS: SOME RECOMMENDATIONS

10

The simple extension of traditional education to broader segments of the population is a woefully inadequate and timid step into the egalitarian age. On the other hand, the bold and revolutionary reforms suggested by some radical reformers are not likely to result in major improvements in an educational system that insists on making its changes in slow evolutionary steps. The recommendations set forth in this chapter are not radical; they do not suggest that we abandon or overthrow the present system. My aim is to recommend the kinds of changes that can start where we are and move forward in a manner that can be accepted by an entrenched educational system and basically conservative students. I hope to suggest some strategies that can be used by administrators in their districts and by teachers in their classrooms to improve the learning opportunities for New Students.

The suggestions to follow are not "proved" or "tested" by research. Rather, they are implied or informed by research. My immersion for more than a year in the data provided by New Students has led me to some convictions in some areas. Nevertheless, this chapter should not be read as a panacea or a dogmatic statement of a single pathway to a better tomorrow. The problems are far too complex for simple solutions. I have had to select for discussion certain things that seemed to me urgent or more closely related to my data. Other people viewing the data presented may be led to other conclusions or to ideas for improvements in areas not covered in this chapter. I sincerely hope that they will be.

New Students—those in the lowest third academically—are telling us in a variety of ways that traditional education must be redesigned for the egalitarian era. They drop out of our traditional schools; they quit listening to lectures; they fail to put forth their best effort; they score low on conventional tests designed to reflect the heart of the traditional academic curriculum; they get low marks for their school performance; their interests, leisure-time activities, and hobbies are "nonacademic"; they fail to develop self-confidence, and they tell us they are nervous and tense in class. They are caught in the impossible bind of wanting to be successful but knowing that they will be required to display the style and values that traditional education will certify.

In moving from the meritocratic era in education to one of egalitarianism, we have not faced up to the fact that equality of educational opportunity requires more than guarantees of equal access to postsecondary education. Access to education that is inappropriate for the development of individual talents may represent nothing more than prolonged captivity in an environment that offers little more than an opportunity to repeat the damaging experiences with school failure that New Students know so well. John Gardner (1961) has described the situation forthrightly: "In the case of the youngster who is not very talented academically, forced continuance of education may simply prolong a situation in which he is doomed to failure. Many a youngstter of low ability has been kept on pointlessly in a school which taught him no vocation, exposed him to continuous failure and then sent him out into the world with a record which convinced employers that he must forever afterward be limited to unskilled or semi-skilled work. This is not a sensible way to conserve human resources" (p. 80).

Neither is it a sensible way to develop individual talents. In a society as complex as ours we need to encourage diversity, and yet we seem unable to move away from our unproductive preoccupation with wanting all children to learn the same things at the same rate. We are in the grip of a "deficiency" conception of New Students. From nursery school to college, we give more attention to correcting the weaknesses of New Students than to developing their strengths. It is easy to cite examples. The purpose of *Sesame Street* is to prepare young children to adapt more easily to the type of education that we happen to offer. At the college level, the primary goal of community college remedial programs is to prepare students for "regular college work" (Appendix C). We ask little more of education than that it prepare young people for the next level of education. When graduates of one level perform well at the next, we count ourselves successful.

John Holt (1971) has criticized the successful *Sesame Street* —not for its accomplishment but for its goal:

> *The operating assumption of the program is probably something like this: poor kids do badly in school because they have a "learning deficit." Schools, and school people, all assume that when kids come to the first grade they will know certain things, be used to thinking and talking in a certain way, and be able to respond to certain kinds of questions and demands. Rich kids on the whole know all this; poor kids on the whole do not. Therefore, if we can just make sure that the poor kids know what the rich kids know by the time they get to school, they will do just as well there as the rich kids. So goes the argument. I don't believe it. Poor kids and rich kids are more alike when they come to school than is commonly believed, and the difference is not the main reason poor kids do badly when they get there. In most ways, schools are rigged against the poor; curing "learning deficits" by Head Start, Sesame Street, or any other means, is not going to change that [p. 72].*

By the time students reach 17 and 18 years of age, their patterns of learning and behaving are much more firmly established than those of four and five year olds, and compensatory programs in community colleges are not going to make many New Students over into traditional students. Furthermore, we have not been able to demonstrate that performance in the traditional discipline-bound curriculum is related to adult success (Warren, 1971). Why, then, do we try so hard to reach a goal that is probably both unattainable and undesirable? Perhaps because the credentials of traditional colleges are important to occupational opportunity (Chapter 7). Understandably, New Students want the key that will unlock such future opportunities. But will the certification via the degree bring equal opportunity to New Students? Probably not. There is growing evidence that the possession of the college degree, as such, is declining in importance. As the degree becomes increasingly common, it becomes less useful as a selective device for employers (Chapter 7); therefore, the possession of college credentials very likely will not provide the relative occupational advantage in the future that it has in the past. Employers who have used college credentials as a screening device will not be able to use them in the same way when increasing proportions of the population possess college degrees. Whether employers will require still higher educational credentials (either higher degrees or higher grades) or whether they will find criteria more relevant to job performance is unknown. It is predictable that the college dropout will have an increasingly difficult time getting a good job. If colleges provide education that fails to meet the needs of New Students, they will still be the ones to make the poorer grades and to drop out of college. In all likelihood, students who have been in the bottom third in conventional elementary and high schools will simply move up to being the bottom third in college unless new ways are found to recognize and develop the diversity of talent that exists in the rapidly expanding pool of candidates for postsecondary education.

New Students, then, will be the losers if we concentrate on access programs that merely assure the entrance of New Students into traditional programs of education. Why can't we, just for once, make new educational programs to fit New Students instead of handing down the old education of traditional students? Perhaps the old education is not as worn out as some traditional students maintain, but like second-hand clothing it is ill-fitting for most New Students.

All of the research presented in this book makes clear that New Students are not the same shape as traditional students. There is little, if any, chance that more than a very few students will be

able to diet or gain weight or develop muscle in some spots and lose
it in others to fit the educational exercise suits of traditional students.
A few tucks and alterations in traditional education, plus a demanding exercise program for New Students, is very unlikely to make
New Students look like traditional students or to fool employers and
the general society into thinking that they are traditional students
—although there are areas of overlap that make some New Students
look like traditional students on some dimensions and vice versa.

A recap of some of the major differences between groups of
New and traditional students follows. New Students, as they are
described in this book (except in Chapters 8 and 9), are those who
score in the lowest third on tests of academic ability. New Student
status should not be equated with low SES or minority ethnicity.
Admittedly the overlap between New Students and the socioeconomically disadvantaged is large, but neither SES nor ethnicity as
such was used in the measurement that formed the basis for the
research classification and description. It is my contention that
children who are constantly in the bottom third of the class throughout their formative years present a particular challenge to educators
at all levels.

As Chapters 5 and 6 show, New Students are positively attracted to careers and prefer to learn things that are tangible and
useful. They tend not to value the academic model of higher education that is prized by faculty, preferring instead a vocational model
that will teach them what they need to know to make a good living.
As Chapter 4 shows, New Students consistently pick the "nonacademic" activities and interests and competencies from among the
lists that we present to them. New Students prefer watching television programs to reading; they prefer working with tools to working with numbers; they feel more competent in using a sewing machine than in reciting long passages from memory. Finally, as
Chapter 3 shows, large and consistent differences exist between the
attitudes and personality characteristics of New Students and traditional students. New Students prefer to learn what others have said
rather than to engage in intellectual questioning. They do not enjoy
intellectual puzzles or the complicated manipulation of ideas and
abstractions. New Students possess a more pragmatic, less questioning, more authoritarian system of values than traditional students.

Upon reading such characterizations of New Students, many sincere social reformers begin immediately to explain why New Students do not look like traditional students. Their explanations usually involve the assumption that if New Students had the advantages of traditional students, they would have the "advantage" of thinking and behaving like traditional students. That may be true, but it is a bit arrogant. Perhaps that brand of arrogance is taught in academe. Kurt Vonnegut, Jr. (1969), observes, "I think about my education sometimes. I went to the University of Chicago for a while after the Second World War. I was a student in the Department of Anthropology. At that time they were teaching that there was absolutely no difference between anybody. They may be teaching that still" (p. 7).

John Gardner (1961) has asked, Can we be equal and excellent too? We might paraphrase the question and ask, Can we be *different* and excellent too? Some people sincerely believe we cannot. The pressure on selective universities to practice open admissions and "special admissions" springs from the fundamental assumption that the education offered by universities is *better* than that offered by state colleges and community colleges. While I agree with the motive of wanting the best possible education for disadvantaged students, I question the means. I suggest that in the long run it is no more desirable for universities to launch special admissions programs for New Students (as defined by low A) than it is for junior colleges to press their faculties for doctor's degrees and research publications. The time is past when a single type of institution can hope to serve the needs of the diverse population now seeking higher education. The notion that universities provide the best in the way of education for New Students is not only a perpetuation of an elitist philosophy in an egalitarian era; it is also probably wrong. Stanley (1971) sums up the arguments against the special recruitment of students who are quite underqualified academically.

It seems likely that trying to compete far above their comfortable level would confine to the easier courses and curricula most students who are quite underqualified academically, thereby limiting their choice. Also, though such students may pass most of their courses with C's and D's, one wonders what they will be learning relative to what they might learn in another college, where their relative level of abilities is average or better. In addition, the negative concept of themselves which they may develop as low men on the academic totem pole must be considered. Perhaps they should be encouraged to attend colleges more geared to their level of academic competence. Not many colleges in the United States are highly selective: at least 2,000 others of all sorts can accommodate most levels of developed ability and achievement [p. 694].

Some New Students are facing a special problem right now. Minority youth, especially, are likely to be offered attractive financial enticements for special admissions programs at prestige institutions and no financial aid at all at community and state colleges. If they hope to attend college, these students may literally be forced into the university. Sowell (1970) is especially critical of what he calls "short-term expediency motives" of selective white institutions that pass over well-qualified blacks in their search for black students with poor academic records in the belief that they are "authentic ghetto types." He writes that the admission of "unprepared black students who are in over their heads academically" and the accompanying tendency of "white faculty members to fudge their grades out of guilt, compassion, or a desire to avoid trouble" is "galling to me as a black man, and . . . should be disturbing to everyone." The long-term effect of such considerations, Sowell maintains, will be to harm the intellectually able black student by using a "double standard which makes his degree look cheap in the market and his grades suspect to those concerned with academic standards. Worst of all, he cannot even have the full confidence within himself that he really earned them" (p. 49).

I suggest that the proper role of the selective universities is not to search out "authentic ghetto types" but rather to conduct an all-out search for academically promising minority students wherever they may be. Increasing numbers of well-qualified minority youth will be graduating from community colleges. These students will need no special attention from the university aside from the assurance that sufficient financial aid will be available to carry them as far as their interest and ability take them. Another source of able minority candidates for higher education has not even been explored. Most minority adults "completed" their educations before the national concern for correcting social injustice. Academically able adults now working in industry or for the government should be encouraged to enter the universities with sufficient financial aid to support their families while they prepare themselves for new careers.

Surely quality education consists not in offering the same thing to all people in a token gesture toward equality but in maximizing the match between the talents of the individual and the teaching resources of the institution. Educational quality is not unidimensional. Colleges can be *different* and excellent too. If New Students are different and not simply less capable academicians than traditional students, then I believe that education for New Students *must* be different in order to be excellent.

On the eve of the egalitarian era, a proposal calling for *different* educational experiences for New Students is easily misunderstood. To some it raises the spectre of "separate but equal," and their concern is a real one that cannot be easily shrugged off. What are our *alternatives?* If everyone is to be offered the *same* type of education, then we must be prepared for the fact that some will do better at it than others. The prestige education of today was designed for, and is perpetuated by, academically oriented faculty and students. It plays to the strengths of traditional students and to the weaknesses of New Students. To claim that equality of *access* leads to equality of educational opportunity to learn is to oversimplify the problem.

If, on the other hand, we are to encourage different kinds of educational experiences for New Students, then we must be absolutely certain that those new approaches to education are first rate, and that they do in fact lead to the fullest possible development of the potential of New Students. The only way I know to do that is to purposefully and deliberately reverse our present priorities in funding. Because it *does* cost more per capita to educate a university student than one in a community college is not to say that it *should.* Education for New Students is expensive, and I believe that it should receive top funding priority if we are to make certain that "different" becomes equated with "best" until there is no longer any danger that it will be equated with "least." Only by offering all people the opportunity to excel in different ways will we ever achieve respect and dignity for all.

A Proposal

Almost everyone agrees that there is an urgent need for educational reform; as yet, however, everyone does *not* agree on the direction that the reformation should take. The main arguments concern the questions of *what* we shall teach and *how* we shall teach it. The question of *whom* we shall teach in postsecondary programs has been answered; and the nation is moving, albeit awkwardly, to implement egalitarianism in the 1970s. (See Chapter 1.)

Most of the modifications in higher education that have been made—or even suggested—to accommodate the egalitarian era are concerned with the structures and forms of college programs rather than the content. Major energies have been directed toward getting New Students into college and keeping them there. Open admissions, special recruitment of disadvantaged students, and financial-aid programs are practices in widespread use throughout the country to attract New Students to college. Remedial courses, counseling, and pass-fail grading are common methods designed to keep New Students in college (Appendix C). Since getting New Students into— and preferably through—college has been the almost single-minded goal, virtually all evaluation of our achievements has been concerned with quoting statistics on increased rates of access and retention.

Only recently have a few scattered voices questioned whether recruitment and retention are really the goals. I think they are not. The goal of educators is to educate. We have, however, sold out to the false goal of certification, and in our eagerness to get degrees in the hands of New Students we are afraid to ask ourselves whether we are *educating* them. We have been told for so long that the quality of education makes little or no difference in the outcome (Coleman, 1966; Astin, 1968) that we have succumbed to fatalistic acceptance of the notion that the credential will do as much for the New Student as the education. There are cheaper and more honest ways to certify.

Let us look first at what certification has meant in the past and what it is likely to mean in the future. In the past, it has meant that the student has had enough persistence and motivation to sit through 128 credit hours of instruction at some kind of institution. Although everyone is well aware that most entering freshmen at highly selective institutions have already accomplished more academically than most graduates of some other four-year institutions, that fact has never really interfered with the public conception that a college graduate is a college graduate. The certificate has also put the college graduate on a higher rung of the occupational ladder. Looming on the horizon now, however, are quite a number of trends that portend changes in the value and process of certification. We have already discussed the practical uselessness of a certificate that the majority of the population possesses. There is also a large body of evidence that performance in the traditional academic curriculum is not very closely related to job performance or to personal happiness or to contributions to society when life situations bear little relationship to the classroom. And finally, the newest form of certification—the external degree—is the exact opposite of the present certification. Advocates of the external degree propose to certify the level of accomplishment regardless of the pathways used to reach it—a quite different concept from that used in certifying the pathways regardless of the final level of accomplishment.

I propose that we reverse the present trends to certify that all students were exposed to the same curriculum, certifying instead that students are high performers in quite disparate areas of accomplishment. There must be no compromise on quality of performance, but it is essential to permit wide individual variation in choice of subjects. This reversal in the emphasis of the educational task is not only more humane but also more realistic. Once we get out of school, we choose the areas in which we will display our competencies. Only in school do we require students to display—more or less publicly—their weaknesses. Human dignity demands the right to be good at something. Indeed, a healthy society is built upon the premise that all citizens will contribute their best talents. The social necessity of emphasizing quality of performance and deemphasizing area of performance has been eloquently expressed by John Gardner (1961): "An excellent plumber is infinitely more admirable than an incompetent philosopher. The society which scorns excellence in plumbing because plumbing is a humble activity and tolerates shoddiness in philosophy because it is an exalted activity will have neither good plumbing nor good philosophy. Neither its pipes nor its theories will hold water" (p. 86).

If, then, excellence is to be the goal, what are the areas in which New Students show potential strength and how can these be matched to the needs of society so that we are developing full individual and societal potential? The world's work can be roughly catalogued under three major headings (see Fine and Heinz, 1958). To put it as directly as possible, we need people to work with people; we need people to work with things; and we need people to work with ideas. I propose that we aim for an ultimate goal in which each citizen attains excellence in one sphere and at least minimal competence in the other two.

Progress in the foreseeable future undoubtedly will be measured by our effectiveness in dealing with human problems and technical problems—areas in which New Students show particular interest and ability. In an advanced society, there will always be a need to push back the frontiers of knowledge by educating and utilizing the talents of people with special gifts in dealing with ideas. There will certainly be a market for traditional students; but we may not need to increase the *proportion* of traditionally trained students. Already there are ominous predictions about the oversupply of traditionally educated young workers. How unfortunate it will be if, in our misguided haste to bestow credentialed equality upon all people, we encourage New Students to enter the ranks of the unemployed by educating them for the glutted academic labor markets when so many New Students show particular strengths and interests in working in the emerging specialties dealing with human problems and those involved with keeping the machinery of the technological age in running condition.

If each student, in addition to developing excellence in one of three spheres of excellence, is to develop at least minimum competence in the other two, he may need special help. The potentially excellent mechanic may need tutoring in English, and the future excellent college professor may need tutoring in the fundamentals of machine repair. Both are handicapped in the modern world without minimum competence in the other's sphere of excellence. And there are few in our society who can survive without at least minimum skills in working with people. Some students are capable of developing outstanding effectiveness and sensitivity to the needs of people and may elect working with people as their sphere of excellence; others may opt for developing minimum or average competency in being able to get along with people.

There is considerable educational merit in promoting the concept of buddy tutoring—"If you tutor me in medieval history, I'll tutor you in auto repair." Many of those who work with peer-tutoring programs have observed that the tutors seem to learn as much as, if not more than, the tutees. Buddy tutoring, then, would have the double advantage of developing the tutor's sphere of excellence while developing the tutee's sphere of competence.

As we contemplate the movement into an egalitarian age, it is intriguing to think about the increased perceptions that might be gained by the academically successful youth from the upper middle class, for example, as he copes with the intricacies of machine repair. In the first place, he discovers that he lacks the vocabulary to know one machine part from another. Furthermore, he may find that while he is trying to use *his* developed skill in reading the repair manual, the instructor is "moving too fast" in a field that does not depend on verbalization. To add to his difficulties, he finds that his parents are totally unable to help him because that kind of learning is not in their background and the materials for learning are not easily available in the home. In other words, a student who has always been successful in school finds himself "educationally disadvantaged," and his symptoms are those that have appeared throughout this book. It may be that such exposure to a field in which he is not expected to be an expert—just competent—would do more than anything else to improve the image of vocational education. But it may also become as essential for all of us to have at least a rudimentary knowledge of the machine age in which we live as it is for all of us to be able to read and to communicate with people.

Consistent with the concept of developing excellence in one of the three spheres is an emphasis upon the evaluation of performance. Contrary to the present trend to abolish or deemphasize evaluation, I propose that *in the sphere of excellence* we renew our efforts to find better ways of testing and grading. The reasons for deemphasizing evaluation—especially, normative testing and grading—arose from analyses of the damaging effects of failure such as that discussed in Chapter 2. But the present proposal does not need to protect against failure, since our goal is to provide enough range so that everyone can succeed—not without effort, however. I believe that the practice of grading has more disadvantages than advantages in elementary school. And I believe that there is more to be lost than gained by an emphasis on grades in the spheres of competence. Pass-fail grading seems highly appropriate in the two spheres of competence. But there are, I believe, good reasons for developing and using a great variety of evaluative techniques in the sphere of excellence. In the first place, the very concept of excellence and the certification of levels of achievement depend upon good evaluation. Second, the individual may be disappointed if, just as he is offered an opportunity to be really good at something, high achievement goes unrecognized; as we have seen, New Students are likely to place particular value on grades and other external measures of evaluation. And third, the student needs to be able to assess his own progress. Evaluations might take the form of performance tests, special projects, oral interviews, or comprehensive examinations. In addition, they might come from a variety of sources—from supervisors of a work-study experience, from people working with a particular project in the community, or from teachers.

Different methods of instruction are expected to be differentially effective depending upon the sphere of study. Lectures and paper-and-pencil tests may well be effective ways of preparing students to work with ideas—although there is now considerable questioning of this venerable assumption. Group work, shop work, and experience in industry and the community may be the best techniques for teaching excellence in the *people* and *things* spheres. Such learning experiences should be given full college credit. They are educational in the best meaning of the term, as long as the emphasis is on learning to perform better or to know more or to deepen appreciation and understanding of the sphere of excellence and one's own place in it.

Remedial Education Revisited

Although I have proposed that education should move in the direction of deemphasizing its concern for weakness and move toward the development of strength, it is apparent that past educational experiences of New Students have resulted in learning handicaps (Chapter 2). The handicaps take two forms: failure to develop competency in such basic tools of modern living as communications skills and mathematics, and the development of attitudinal blockages to the learning process itself. Of the two, the latter is much more serious.

The first business of educational programs for New Students should be to provide a reorientation to learning itself. Once the student is comfortable in learning situations, he is free to pursue learning in his sphere of interest and talent. The student who knows how to tackle the job of learning new things may choose to apply his skill to traditional tasks of education or he may apply it to nontraditional studies.

Both the theory and the research presented in this book lead to the conclusion that New Students approach learning tasks in a different manner from that used by their more successful peers. Holt (1970) reached the same conclusion through observation: "Until recently it had not occurred to me that poor students thought differently about their work than good students; I assumed they thought the same way, only less skillfully. Now it begins to look as if the expectation and fear of failure, if strong enough, may lead children to act and think in a special way, to adopt strategies different from those of more confident children" (p. 48).

Acceptance of the fear-of-failure hypothesis advanced in Chapter 2 as a major cause of learning difficulties has a number of implications for teaching New Students to higher education. Teaching youth who have learned to fear failure in school instead of to seek achievement calls for different instructional approaches from those used in traditional education. According to the theory, achievement-motivated persons are most likely to approach new learning tasks of intermediate difficulty, where the chances of success are about 50–50. Thus they are ready to tackle the task that is just a little ahead of their present skills. This approach describes what we ordinarily think of as efficient learning—moving to progressively higher levels of accomplishment in small increments. For the failure-threatened individual, the task of intermediate difficulty is most likely to be avoided in favor of nonthreatening tasks of assured success or of no probability of accomplishment. From a learning standpoint, there is nothing to be gained from following either of these tendencies. To do something you already know how to do is not learning. Neither is trying something that you cannot possibly do. The problem, then, is how to move the failure-threatened individual into the "learning" range of behaviors, into approaching tasks that are just a little beyond his capacity, so that he has to stretch or grow to attain them.

The lesson that the New Students have learned in school is that giving the wrong answer is painful—unless you can convince yourself that it doesn't matter. Community colleges have diagnosed the learning problem correctly. "Lack of effort; has quit trying" ranked first among the perceived obstacles to learning for low-achieving students (Appendix C). How, then, can we convince students that there will be no pain in trying or that they can deal with the pain of being wrong?

A few community colleges (only 3 per cent—see Appendix C) have experimented with "guaranteed-success" programs. Although this term is a misnomer for reasons that will be discussed later, the concept is sound. It involves starting the student where he wants to start—with something he knows he can do. The method hinges on good diagnosis and on careful management of the learning process. Basically, the student is assigned tasks one or two levels below his tested ability and, as he gains self-confidence, he is gradually moved to more difficult assignments. The student's tendency, according to the theory, will be to persevere at the easy tasks. This kind of "guaranteed success" is not success in the long run. The rewarding feeling of achievement comes not from doing something that you know you can do but from doing something that you thought you might not be able to do.

The experience of accomplishment always involves risk. When we say that achievement-motivated personalities approach a task at the 50–50 level of probability of success, we mean that there is as much risk of failure as there is chance of success in the beginning. To change a failure-threatened student into an achievement-oriented learner involves a fundamental change of attitude. It means that the learner must become eager to test himself instead of becoming motivated to find ways of avoiding the test of personal competency. It means that the student must become curious about himself and what he can do instead of being afraid to find out. Most important, it means that the challenge to the learner is to improve upon his own past record—to seek out the task that is just a little more difficult than what he has already accomplished. In this definition of school learning, comparison with fellow students becomes irrelevant as the student seeks the development of his own competencies and the skills of assessing his own progress.

The goal of reorienting the New Student to learning is to change attitudes, but the student must also be given ample practice in learning. Instructors in reorientation courses have a special need for understanding the learning process, but their task is more complicated. They need to feel as well as to know the learning problems of New Students. Their first task is to develop in the student a curiosity about his own capacities and a willingness to take risks to his ego to find out. First and foremost, the counselor or tutor must believe that the student can perform the task. There are two basic clues to the student that a teacher lacks confidence in him. One is to quit trying to teach him. Teachers, too, can have a fear-of-failure syndrome. If they believe that all efforts to teach New Students will fail, then they may go through the motions, but they have really quit trying—just as students quit trying in the face of impending failure. This problem is most likely to occur among teachers who are *assigned* to remedial classes. Fortunately this practice is becoming less common, and almost half of the community colleges now restrict teaching in developmental programs to volunteers who express interest (Appendix C).

But another problem plagues some sincere and dedicated volunteers, who are motivated largely by sympathy for disadvantaged youth and by social concern for past injustices. They want to see the student get the "goodies" that have been denied him in the past (credits, degrees, job opportunities); but in their kindness they deny him the educational experiences involved in earning them. The problem may be especially difficult for whites working with black students. Trent (1970) writes, "Unfortunately, when predominantly white institutions or white individuals do begin to assist the black community or individual, they tend to overassist. This act of benevolence often becomes repulsively condescending in the eyes of the student or degrading to his ability" (p. 6).

Those who overassist the New Student show the same basic lack of confidence in his learning capacity as those who have quit trying to teach him. "Overassisters" may be more dangerous in the long run because they deny the student the opportunity to take the real risks that learning involves. The reorientation to learning comes from the student's knowledge that, *through his own effort,* he has accomplished a difficult task. It cannot come from telling him he is doing fine—when he is not or when he is learning tasks at a level far below his capacity. Although research generally shows the efficacy of praise, Holt (1970) has raised some questions about its excessive use even with quite young children. "Do children really need so much praise?" he asks. "When a child after a long struggle finally does the cube puzzle, does he need to be told that he has done well? Doesn't he know, without being told, that he has accomplished something?" (p. 69).

Although the role of constant evaluation and feedback in learning is hard to overemphasize, students know when they have done their best. The teacher who accepts poor performance (basically because he or she does not think the student can do better—or thinks that because of past injustices the student should not have to do better) is doing a grave disservice to New Students. In the final analysis, the teacher who cares must have enough teaching skill and enough confidence in the student to create the environment and situations that require the student's best efforts.

It would be ideal if each student could design a learning task of his own choosing, but realistically it is desirable to develop a number of tasks very carefully and let the student choose which tasks he will undertake. Teachers from the three spheres of excellence should develop learning projects for use in reorientation-to-learning classes. In most cases, the learning models can do double duty by serving both the remedial and reorientation—the cognitive and affective— functions that are necessary to overcome the learning handicaps of New Students.

It is especially important that the learning projects be models of good learning. Ralph Tyler (1970) describes seven conditions required for effective learning that may be useful as a checklist in developing models. Summarized, they are as follows: (1) The student must have a clear idea of what he is trying to learn. He needs concrete examples of persons doing what he is expected to learn in order to guide his own efforts. (2) The motivation of the student must be strong enough to impel him to an initial attempt and then to continue the practice. (3) Students must be helped to focus their efforts on the significant features of the behavior they are seeking to master. (4) There must be ample opportunity for practice in appropriate situations that are meaningful to the student. (5) The student must be provided with feedback on his performance. Practice without specific information about specific inadequacies simply perpetuates the inadequacies. (6) There must be a reward system such that students derive satisfaction from improving their performance. Measurable improvement in the significant features of behavior is one of the most satisfactory rewards. (7) The sequential organization of learning experiences is essential for learning complex and difficult things.

If these requirements for effective learning sound like "behavioral objectives" and "criterion-referenced evaluation," they are the fundamental principles upon which some of the new behavioral objectivists are building. The present behavioral bandwagon has its articulate critics (Silberman, 1970, for one) and justifiably so, but lessons consisting of discrete tasks with measurable outcomes that are immediately available to inform the student of his learning progress are ideal for use in reorienting New Students to learning. Ideally, students could complete several learning projects, involving different kinds of skills, thus giving them some experience on which to base later learning preferences. Some may realize that they prefer working with things or people, whereas others may discover that they have talent for traditional academic studies. The choice of the type of project should be left to the student, but the standards of performance are non-negotiable. They must be the best the student is capable of.

Students in reorientation-to-learning classes should learn something about learning processes. They should know, for example, that learning is not 100 per cent success. When that point has been reached, we may say that something *has been* learned, but learning is in progress only when there are things we cannot do or do not know. In the learning of skills, for example, when a task is performed correctly seven out of ten times, the next goal might be the achievement of success eight out of ten times; or learning might be directed toward moving to a more difficult level and achieving success only six out of ten times. In the first instance, the student is learning the task; in the second, he is learning how to learn—how to advance to increasingly difficult levels involving greater risks of failure. Both processes are essential to the full development of talent.

The better the student understands the process of learning, the better he can monitor his own progress. The monitoring function should gradually move from teacher to student, and ultimately the student should accept responsibility for his learning progress. When the student can direct his own learning, he has learned the most important lesson that education can teach him. Lifelong learning will be a requirement of the future.

As a matter of fact, the most rapidly growing segment of American education is the "educational periphery," a term used by Moses (1970) to describe systematic educational activities that go on outside the educational core of elementary, secondary, and higher education. Included in the periphery are *programs sponsored by employers*—business, government, and industry—to upgrade the capability of employees; *proprietary schools,* usually run for profit and including beauty schools, computer training, refrigeration schools; *antipoverty programs* such as the Job Corps and Manpower Training and Development Centers; *correspondence courses; educational television,* which is beginning to perform educational functions for all ages—from *Sesame Street* to *Sunrise Semester; adult-education programs* ranging from evening courses to neighborhood and social-action groups concerned with "affective" learning. In 1970, the numbers of people pursuing structured educational activities in the educational core stood at about 64 million, whereas the number in the periphery was estimated at 60 million. By 1976, the number in the core will be approximately 67 million, compared to 82 million in the rapidly growing periphery (Moses, 1970).

Education in America *has* moved out of the confines of the "regular school system," and these new opportunities will probably create entire new categories of "New Students to Higher Education." With little or no attention from the educational establishment, millions of citizens are creating their own lifelong-learning models of education, and we may look forward to the day when education is not something that should be completed before age 25. In the final analysis, enabling people to learn—however, whenever, and whatever they have a need or desire to learn—is the aim of all education.

References

ASTIN, A. W. "Undergraduate Achievement and Institutional 'Excellence.' " *Science,* 1968.

COLEMAN, J. S., CAMPBELL, E. Q., HOBSON, C. J., MC PARTLAND, J., MOOD, A. M., WEINFELD, F. D., YORK, R. L. *Equality of Educational Opportunities.* Washington, D.C.: Government Printing Office, 1966.

FINE, S. A., AND C. A. HEINZ. "The Functional Occupational Classification Structure." *Personnel and Guidance Journal,* 1958, *37,* 180–192.

GARDNER, J. *Excellence: Can We Be Equal and Excellent Too?* New York: Harper & Row, 1961.

HOLT, J. *How Children Fail.* New York: Dell, 1970.

————. "Big Bird, Meet Dick and Jane." *Atlantic,* May 1971, pp. 72–78.

MOSES, S. "Notes on the Learning Force." *Notes on the Future of Education.* Syracuse: Educational Policy Research Center, February 1970, *1*(2), 6–8.

SILBERMAN, C. E. *Crisis in the Classroom.* New York: Random House, 1970.

SOWELL, T. *New York Times Magazine,* December 13, 1970, p. 36.

STANLEY, J. C. "Predicting College Success of the Educationally Disadvantaged." *Science,* February 19, 1971, pp. 640–647.

TRENT, W. T. *College Compensatory Programs for Disadvantaged Students.* Report 3. Washington, D.C.: ERIC Clearinghouse on Higher Education, September 1970.

TYLER, R. W. "Academic Excellence and Equal Opportunity." In F. Harcleroad, ed., *Issues of the Seventies.* San Francisco: Jossey-Bass, 1970, pp. 166–183.

VONNEGUT, K., JR. *Slaughterhouse Five.* New York: Delacorte Press, 1969.

WARREN, J. R. "Current Grading Practices." *College and University Bulletin.* Research Report No. 3. Washington, D.C.: American Association for Higher Education, 1971.

CHARACTERISTICS OF
FOUR MAJOR
DATA SOURCES

A

Project TALENT

SAMPLE

Project TALENT data represent a probability sample of approximately 5 per cent of the public, private, and parochial high schools in the country. The total TALENT sample included 400,000 students in grades 9–12 in 1,353 schools. Stratification variables included geographical area, size of senior class, retention ratio, and school category (public, parochial, or private). Extensive technical corrections have been applied to the data with the intent of making the sample as nationally representative as possible. The sample used in this book represents approximately 10 per cent of the 62,602 twelfth graders tested in the spring of 1960. The 1961 and 1965 follow-up data have been weighted for nonrespondent bias. Project TALENT comes closer than any other data bank used herein to approximating a nationally representative sample.

INSTRUMENTS

The Project TALENT two-day battery consisted of instruments in the following broad categories: (1) Information tests of knowledge acquired in and out of school (38 scores). (2) Language and mathematics aptitude and ability tests (13 scores). (3) Tests of specific aptitudes, including creativity, mechanical and abstract reasoning, and visualization (15 scores). (4) Tests of specific clerical, computational, and perceptual abilities (4 scores). (5) Student Information Blank regarding family background, school experiences, plans (394 items). (6) Interest inventory (17 scales). (7) Student-activities inventory (10 temperament scales).

CRITERION INSTRUMENT

The General Academic Aptitude Composite (Code No. C–002) was used to divide the TALENT sample into thirds. Twelfth-grade norms gave the following cutting scores: top third, 596 and above; middle third, 488–595; lowest third, 487 and below.

The General Academic Aptitude Composite "includes tests of verbal and numerical facility; verbal, quantitative, and non-verbal-nonquantitative reasoning; and specific information in English and mathematics. It is a highly reliable measure and is likely to predict overall scholastic achievement rather closely" (Flanagan et al., 1964).

The TALENT sample of lowest-third students appears similar to the other three on the socioeconomic indices of father's education and father's occupation (see Appendix B). Girls score slightly lower on the General Academic Aptitude Composite than do boys; hence girls are somewhat overrepresented in the TALENT New Student Group.

ADDITIONAL INFORMATION

FLANAGAN, J. C., et al. *Design for a Study of American Youth.* Boston: Houghton Mifflin, 1962.

——————. *The American High School Student.* Pittsburgh: Project TALENT Office, University of Pittsburgh, 1964.

——————. *The Project TALENT Data Bank.* Pittsburgh: Project TALENT Office, University of Pittsburgh, March 1965.

Growth Study

SAMPLE

The Growth Study sample was designed to represent the range of United States school systems with respect to geographical region, size, and proportion of graduates who attend college. It is not, however, a probability sample; and over half of the subjects resided in one of three large cities: Akron, Ohio; Erie, Pennsylvania; and Oakland, California. The urban bias may account for the large proportion of students continuing their education beyond high school relative to the other samples used.

The basic Growth Study sample consisted of 8,891 students in seventeen cities. The students were first tested in 1961 as seventh graders. Only those students for whom data were available for the 1961, 1963, 1965, and 1967 testings were included in the present study. This represents 3,220 students, who remained in the study consistently from seventh grade through nine months after high school graduation. The determination of New Students was made on the basis of test scores achieved by the eleventh-grade group in the fall of 1965.

INSTRUMENTS

The Growth Study fifteen-hour battery consists of the following: (1) Sequential Tests of Educational Progress (STEP): includes six tests in the four major academic areas of communications (reading, writing, and listening), social studies, science, and mathematics. (2) School and College Ability Tests (SCAT): a seventy-minute academic-aptitude test with three scores: Verbal, Quantitative, and Total. (3) Background and Experience Questionnaire (BEQ): a 177-item questionnaire about home environment, recreation, reading, hobbies, attitudes, and goals. (4) Tests of General Information (TGI): a forty-minute 120-item test of general factual knowledge that is available to the informed public. It tests information in medicine, science, arts, humanities, entertainment, and public affairs. (5) Senior Questionnaire: a brief eight-item questionnaire given to seniors to get information about their immediate, post–high school plans. (6) Other cognitive measures used in the Growth

Study (but not included in the present analysis) are the PSAT and the College Board English Composition and American History Achievement Tests.

CRITERION INSTRUMENT

The total score of the SCAT test was used to divide the Growth Study sample into thirds. It is a reliable (0.95) test of academic aptitude, correlating about 0.55 with school marks in grade eleven. Cutting scores, based on eleventh-grade norms, were as follows: Lowest third, 260 and below; middle third, 261–270; upper third, 271 and above. Females are overrepresented in the low-scoring group, primarily because of low quantitative scores. Appendix B shows the Growth Study New Students similar to other New Students on socioeconomic variables, but educational aspirations appear somewhat higher than other groups.

ADDITIONAL INFORMATION

HILTON, THOMAS L. *Annotated Bibliography of Growth Study Papers.* Princeton: Educational Testing Service, May 1969.

School and College Ability Tests. *Technical Report.* Princeton: Educational Testing Service, 1957.

SCOPE. School to College: Opportunities for Postsecondary Education

SAMPLE

For the 1966 SCOPE twelfth grade sample used in these analyses, secondary schools were used as the sampling units. The goal of the SCOPE research staff was to obtain as representative a sample as possible of high school students within four states showing diversity in the proportion of young people entering college. The states and the number of high school seniors participating in the 1966 survey were California, 7,567; Illinois, 8,600; Massachusetts, 6,335; and North Carolina, 11,377. Because of difficulty in obtaining the cooperation of metropolitan school districts, urban students are somewhat underrepresented in the SCOPE sample. This bias may be responsible in part for the rather low college-attendance rates of the SCOPE sample when compared with other national data. The sample used in the analyses throughout this book is the four-state composite consisting of some 33,000 students.

INSTRUMENTS

The SCOPE instrument battery consisted of the following measures used for students who were in the twelfth grade in 1966: (1) Academic Ability Test (AAT): a fifty-minute traditional test of academic ability. It correlates very highly with the School and College Ability Test (SCAT) and gives verbal, mathematical, and total scores. (2) Occupational Preferences: a 122-item list of occupations for which the student is asked to indicate extent of liking. (3) Activity Preferences: an 83-item test of activities for which the student is asked to indicate the extent of liking. (4) Student Attitudes: a 55-item inventory of attitude statements, with scales labeled Autonomy, Thinking Introversion, Theoretical Orientation, Deferment of Satisfaction, Active-Passive, and Intellectual Predisposition. (5) Student Questionnaire: a 192-item questionnaire inquiring about home and school experiences as well as future aspirations and plans. (6) College Questionnaire: a 143-item questionnaire administered one year after high school graduation (1967 for this cohort) to students attending a postsecondary institution of education. Items concern reaction to college, interests, and aspirations. (7) Parents' Questionnaire: a 12-item questionnaire, mailed to parents of SCOPE participants, inquiring mostly about parental financial support for postsecondary education.

CRITERION INSTRUMENT

The Cooperative Academic Ability Test is a special form of the School and College Ability Tests (SCAT). It is a 45-minute test of general academic ability consisting of verbal and mathematical sections. The test has a reliability of 0.90 and a correlation of 0.56 with rank in graduating class for the norms sample (Cooperative Academic Ability Test, 1964).

The total score was used to divide the SCOPE sample into thirds. Cutting scores were based on the SCOPE four-state composite norms and were as follows: Lowest third, 42 and below; middle third, 43 to 58; and top third, 59 and above. Females were overrepresented in the lowest third because of lower female test scores. Mean scores on the AAT were 53 for boys and 49 for girls, with standard deviations of 20 and 18 respectively.

ADDITIONAL INFORMATION

Cooperative Academic Ability Test. *Handbook.* Princeton: Cooperative Test Division, Educational Testing Service, 1964.

TILLERY, D., B. SHERMAN, AND D. DONOVAN. SCOPE (School to College: Opportunities for Postsecondary Education). Research Proposal Submitted to the College Entrance Examination Board. Berkeley: Center for Research and Development in Higher Education, University of California, October 30, 1965.

—————. *SCOPE Four-State Profile, Grade Twelve, 1966.* Prepared for the College Entrance Examination Board. Berkeley: Center for Research and Development in Higher Education, University of California, 1966.

TILLERY, D. *School to College: Distribution and Differentiation of Youth.* Prepared for College Entrance Examination Board. Berkeley: Center for Research and Development in Higher Education, University of California, 1971.

Comparative Guidance and Placement Program (CGP)

SAMPLE

The Comparative Guidance and Placement Program is a new battery of tests and questionnaires offered by the College Entrance Examination Board to two-year colleges. The sample used herein consisted of 23,719 students to whom the CGP battery was administered by forty-five two-year colleges voluntarily subscribing to the CGP program. The 14,939 men and 8,780 women in the sample took the tests between July and October of 1969. Some colleges administered the battery to students who were planning to enter in the fall; others, to enrolled students. The CGP sample differs in two major ways from the other three samples used herein. It consists of junior college students (or planned entrants), and it is not designed to represent anything except users of the CGP tests.

The sample, however, looks reasonably representative of two-year-college students. Table 33 gives some information about the

Table 33.   CHARACTERISTICS OF CGP COLLEGES—1969

Test N	Region	No. Colleges	Control Public	Private	Size Under 1,000	Over 1,000
2,986	Midwest	8	6	2	2	6
11,504	East	17	13	4	9	8
4,841	West	6	5	1	2	4
4,754	South	14	12	2	8	6
24,085[a]	Total	45	36	9	21	24

[a] Because of missing data on some student records, the number in the sample used herein is 23,719.

characteristics of the colleges participating in the summer/fall 1969 administration of the CGP.

INSTRUMENTS

The 1969 CGP battery is basically a guidance program designed to help two-year colleges in the guidance and placement of individuals. It consists of a set of instruments focused on experiences, interests, and special abilities. The tests may be described under three categories: (1) Biographical inventory: a 65-item questionnaire about plans, backgrounds, and attitudes. Special sets of items give scores indicating Financial Need, Academic Motivation, and Vocational Motivation. (2) Comparative Interest Index: Students are asked to indicate the extent of their interest in each of 176 activities related to eleven academic and vocational fields such as biology, business, home economics, and engineering technology. (3) Tests of special abilities: a battery of six tests of basic skills and special abilities, measuring such traditional skills as reading, written communications, and fundamental mathematics and nontraditional skills such as short-term memory and nonverbal reasoning.

CRITERION INSTRUMENT

The Sentences Test was used to divide the CGP sample into thirds. It is a twenty-minute forty-item test designed to reveal mastery of grammatical rules and usage. Students are asked to identify the faulty component among a number of underlined elements in a sentence. This test was chosen because past research revealed it to be the best predictor of junior college grades. Median validities across curriculums and institutions range from 0.23 to 0.61. (See Research Report for Georgia Vocational-Technical Schools, 1969; and CGP *Progress Report,* 1968.) The reliability is reported as 0.82. While the Sentences Test has the advantage of being unspeeded, it has the disadvantage of favoring females strongly. The mean for males is 49 and for females 54. The bias had the effect of making a heavily male sample (63 per cent of the total CGP sample) even more heavily male (71 per cent) when the lowest third was considered. Most of the CGP data are reported separately for males and females except in situations where differences between the sexes are minor.

ADDITIONAL INFORMATION

College Entrance Examination Board. *Comparative Guidance and Placement Program Interpretative Manual.* Princeton: College Entrance Examination Board, 1969–70.

Educational Testing Service. *Research Report for Georgia Vocational-Technical Schools.* Princeton: Educational Testing Service, 1969.

―――――. *Progress Report, Comparative Guidance and Placement Program.* Princeton: College Entrance Examination Board, 1968.

Table 34 is a time design for the four major data banks discussed here.

Table 34. TIME DESIGN FOR FOUR MAJOR DATA BANKS

YEAR OF DATA COLLECTIONS

	1960	1961	1962	1963	1964	1965	1966	1967	1968	1969

TALENT

12th grade[a]	one-year follow-up			five-year follow-up
$N = 62,602$	$N = 49,470$			$N = 20,965$

GROWTH

7th grade	9th grade	11th grade[a]	12th grade	one-year follow-up
$N = 8,891$	$N = 8,724$	$N = 7,383$	$N = 5,891$	$N = 4,425$

SCOPE

12th grade[a]	college follow-up
$N = 33,965$	$N = 10,590$

CGP

two-year colleges[a]
$N = 23,719$

[a] Criterion group for determination of New Students.

KEY CHARACTERISTICS
OF NEW STUDENTS

B

Some information about the four major sources of data used throughout this book may be gained by a comparison of data on selected student characteristics. The figures reported in Table 35 represent the percentages of New Students (lowest third on the measure of academic aptitude) possessing the given characteristic. Categories have been adjusted insofar as possible to facilitate comparison. Differences are due to many things—date of the study, nature of the sample, the phrasing of the item, and the nature of the instrument used to categorize the total sample into thirds.

Table 35. COMPARATIVE DATA FOR SELECTED CHARACTERISTICS OF *New Students* FROM THE FOUR MAJOR DATA SOURCES

	TALENT	SCOPE	GROWTH	CGP
Date	12th grade, 1960 follow-up 1961, 1965	12th grade, 1966 follow-up 1967	11th grade, 1965 follow-up 1967	13th grade, 1969
	Per Cent	*Per Cent*	*Per Cent*	*Per Cent*
Male Sex				
Lowest Third	45	43	39	71
Total Sample	47	49	44	63
Race	Not available	Not available in '66–'67	Not available	*Per Cent*
				Am. Ind. 2
				Caucasian 56
				Mex./Sp. 4
				Negro/Black 23
				Oriental 7
				No response 8
	Per Cent	*Per Cent*	*Per Cent*	*Per Cent*
Father's Education				
Grade school	37	26	11	20
High school	34	39	57	39

Father's Occupation

Group 6

Vocation/Some college
College grad.	3
More than B.A.	3
N.R. & don't know	18

Summary: 71% of fathers high school graduate or less

	Per Cent
Prof. & exec.	12
Low exec./Mgr.	4
Sales	2
Clerical/Office	19
Skilled	10
Service	2
Semiskilled	10
Unskilled	27
Farmer	11
Don't know	2

Summary: 60% Blue Collar

Group 9

Vocation/Some college
College grad.	4
More than B.A.	2
N.R. & don't know	20

Summary: 65% of fathers high school graduate or less

	Per Cent
Prof. & exec.	8
Low exec./Mgr.	12
Sales	5
Office	3
Skilled	36
Service	8
Unskilled	16
N.R. & don't know	12

Summary: 60% Blue Collar

Group 10

Vocation/Some college
College grad.	8
More than B.A.	2
Don't know	12

Summary: 68% of fathers high school graduate or less

	Per Cent
Prof. & exec.	12
Low exec./Mgr.	15
Sales	4
Skilled	16
Semiskilled	28
Service }	
Clerical }	18
Unskilled }	
Other	7

Summary: 62% Blue Collar

Group 12

Vocation/Some college
College grad.	5
More than B.A.	3
No response	20

Summary: 59% of fathers high school graduate or less

	Per Cent
Prof. & exec.	8
Low exec./Mgr.	11
Sales and office	7
Skilled	18
Service	6
Semiskilled	17
Unskilled	11
No response	22

Summary: 52% Blue Collar, but high N.R. rate

Table 35 (Cont.) Comparative Data for Selected Characteristics of *New Students* from the Four Major Data Sources

	TALENT	SCOPE	GROWTH	CGP
High School Grades		Expected teacher rating	Senior rank in class (12th grade)	

TALENT

	Per Cent
All A's	3
Mostly A's	8
Mostly A's & B's	24
Mostly B's & C's	43
Mostly C's & D's	21
Mostly D's & below	2

Summary: 35% had above B average

SCOPE — Expected teacher rating

	Per Cent
Excellent	2
Good	20
Average	60
Poor, but passing	13
Not passing	1
No response	4

Summary: 22% above average

GROWTH — Senior rank in class (12th grade)

	Per Cent
Top 10%	1
75-90 percentile	5
50-74 percentile	10
25-49 percentile	29
Below 25th percentile	55

Summary: 16% in upper half

CGP

	Per Cent
Mostly A's	0
Half A's, half B's	3
Mostly B's	10
Half B's, half C's	34
Mostly C's	30
Half C's, half D's	13
Mostly D's	1
Mostly D's & below	0
No response	6

Summary: 13% had above B average

Educational Plans

Likely to attend	Per Cent	Plans after high school	Per Cent	Plans after high school (12th grade Q)	Per Cent	Plan to complete	Per Cent
Four-year college	15	Four-year college	10	Four-year	20	Four years or more	31
Junior college	9	Junior college	11	Two-year	20	Two-year transfer	11
Not going	48	Voc. school	18	Other training	17	Two-year occup.	24
Don't know	16	Military	7	Military	7	One-year program	7
No response	13	Full-time job	25	Full-time job	29	No special plans	15
		Job & school	7	Housewife	3	Other	6
		Marriage	3	Other	5	No response	6
		Other, none, and Don't know	16				

Summary: 24% plan two-year or four-year college

Summary: 21% plan two-year or four-year college

Summary: 40% plan two-year or four-year college

Summary: 66% plan completion of two- or four-year program

QUESTIONNAIRE ON DEVELOPMENTAL SERVICES

C

The Questionnaire was mailed in March 1970 to a 20 per cent random sample of two-year colleges listed in the 1969 American Association of Junior Colleges *Directory*. Responses were received from 141 colleges for a 78 per cent return.

Tabulations are presented in percentages except for items 4 and 5, which called for rankings. Rank orders for these items were determined by adding the numbers of respondents who placed the alternative first or second in importance, and rank-ordering the totals.

1. The provisions colleges are making for poorly prepared students range all the way from hiring an additional counselor to developing a full program of recruitment, courses, counseling, etc. Does your college have any special provisions for students who do not meet the traditional academic requirements for college work?

   80% Yes.

   20% No. If your answer is "No," you need not complete the questionnaire. If, however, you would like a summary of the data tabulations, please sign your name at the end of the questionnaire and return it in the envelope provided.

2. Please place an x in the box by *any* of the following that describe special services offered at your college *this year*.

64%   Efforts to recruit students who would not ordinarily seek a college education.

76%   Financial aids designed especially for disadvantaged students.

61%   Special counseling programs.

92%   Remedial or developmental courses to upgrade verbal or other academic skills.

20%   A total program of recruitment, counseling, courses, etc., with a director.

Other.

3. If you have a special program for educationally disadvantaged students, what is its title?

4. What do you see as the major obstacle to learning for low-achieving students? Please rank, using a 1 for the most important, 2 for the next most important, etc.

7   Low intelligence.

2   Poor home background.

3   Poor elementary and secondary schooling.

1   Lack of effort; has quit trying.

4   Fear of failure.

5   More interested in nonacademic matters such as car, sports, job.

6   The necessity of a job prevents adequate time and energy for study.

Other.

5. Please rank the following broad goals of your college's efforts to educate underprepared students in order of importance:

1   To prepare students for regular college work.

2   To provide skills for job and family responibilities.

5   To provide for the needs of minority group students.

4   To assist in developing nonacademic talents of the individual.

3   To change attitudes toward self and school.

Other.

6. Do you offer any kind of remedial or compensatory courses?

95%   Yes.

5%   No.   If your answer is "No," skip to question 13.

7. Approximately what proportion of the full-time student body is enrolled in remedial courses?

40% Less than 10 per cent.
39% Between 10 and 25 per cent.
16% Between 25 and 50 per cent.
3% More than 50 per cent.

8. What proportion of those taking remedial courses are members of racial minorities?

64% Less than 25 per cent.
19% Between 25 and 50 per cent.
10% Between 50 and 75 per cent.
5% More than 75 per cent.

9. Are remedial courses required for certain students?

79% Yes.
19% No.

10. How is eligibility for remedial courses determined? (Answer all that apply.)

75% Test scores   (Below what percentile? on what test?)
50% High school grades   (Below $C+$, C, $C-$, $D+$, D, $D-$)
                                    (please circle)
54% Interview
     Other.

11. Do remedial courses carry

25% No credit.
29% Nondegree credit.
32% Degree credit.

12. Approximately what proportion of students enrolled in remedial courses later enter regular college courses at your or other institutions?

11% Less than 10 per cent.
11% Between 10 and 25 per cent.
12% Between 25 and 50 per cent.
45% More than half.
18% Don't know.

Special Features of Developmental Efforts

Listed below are some techniques that are frequently used in helping poorly prepared students. Please make an X in the box by those activities that are in use *this year* at your college.

13. Recruitment of students

70% Visits to high schools in disadvantaged areas.
60% Specific requests to high school counselors.

58%   Work with community agencies and leaders.

52%   Use of students to help in recruiting.

24%   Use of a special recruitment program such as TALENT Search, NSSFNS, Upward Bound.

14%   Other recruitment techniques.

14. Admissions

81%   Open admissions.

4%   Attempt to attract a certain number from racial minorities— use of a quota.

19%   Relaxation of test scores or high school grades for under-prepared students.
Other.

15. Financial aid

63%   Available to needy students regardless of academic standing; for instance, may retain grant while on probation.

71%   "Need" used as a major criterion of eligibility for funds.

59%   Use of a federally funded program designed for disadvantaged students; EOP.

38%   College has some funds of its own for poorly prepared students.
Other.

16. Counseling services

22%   Separate counseling office for underprepared students.

33%   Use of group interaction or group counseling.

36%   Program of teacher counselors.

17%   Use of students as counselors.

40%   Diagnostic testing.

12%   Other.

17. Academic adjustments

58%   Remedial students carry a lighter course load.

27%   Nonpunitive grading; for instance, pass–no pass.

58%   Remedial classes smaller than regular classes.
Other.

18. Instructional methods

22%   Team teaching.

45%   Emphasis on audio-visual aids.

36%   Skills centers.

36%   Tutoring by fellow students.

44%   Programmed instruction.

3%   "Guaranteed-success" programs.

   7%   Practicum accompanies academic (for instance, New Careers).

   5%   Gaming or psychodrama.

 21%   Use of materials drawn from black and other ethnic cultures.

 31%   "Pacing" methods; emphasis on achievement regardless of time taken.

   7%   Other.

19. Physical facilities

 21%   Separate office for the program.

   4%   Separate student lounge available.

        Other.

20. Special help with studies.

 48%   Precollege or summer programs.

 39%   Additional intensified study for underprepared students while enrolled in regular classes.

   8%   Other.

21. Faculty

 47%   Instruction of remedical courses restricted to teachers expressing interest.

 50%   Most remedial teachers have some special training for work with underprepared students.

   9%   Group-sensitivity sessions for faculty.

 37%   All expenses paid for attendance at off-campus conferences, workshops.

 16%   On-campus in-service training for remedial instructors.

 13%   Emphasis on use of racial minorities for faculty.

        Other.

22. Evaluation

 55%   Measurement of changes in test scores.

 36%   Measurement of changes in student attitudes.

 50%   Follow-up of students on the job or in college.

 30%   Formal collection of faculty and student reactions to program.

   4%   Other.

23. What do you regard as particular strengths or distinctions of your program?

24. What problems concerned with education of the underprepared seem to you most in need of attention?

     If you have any written materials concerning your program, I would appreciate receiving them. Thank you for your cooperation.

INDEX

A

Academic ability: among college graduates, 104; among New Students, 164–166; of students entering college, 120–123; of women, 135–138

Academic Ability Test (AAT), 179, 180

Activity preferences, student, 60, 61, 62. *See also* Interest profiles

ADAMS, W., 118, 119

Admission to college, 25, 26; of minority students, 160–163 *passim*

ADORNO, T. W., 35

American Association for Higher Education (AAHE), 128

American Indians. *See* Minorities

American College Testing Program (ACT), 141

American Council on Education (ACE), 61, 87, 89, 125–143 *passim*

ANASTASI, A., 137

ANDERSON, S., 58, 59

Aristocrats, 1, 2, 3, 9

Aspirations: SCOPE figures on, 190; of students for going to college, 117–120; of women going to college, 144–145

Assistance, student requests for, 77–81, 84

ASTIN, A. W., 61, 128, 129, 163

ATKINSON, J. W., 22, 23, 30

Attitudes: of high-achieving students, 48–54; of students toward college, 73–77; of students toward past education, 72–73

B

Background and Experience Questionnaire (BEQ), 177

BALL, S., 58

BAYER, A., 115, 117, 119, 125, 127

Behavioral objectives, 172

BERG, I., 113

BINZEN, P., 15, 32

Blacks in colleges, 12, 63. *See also* Minorities

Blue-collar students, 40–47 *passim*, 86, 115

BOGATZ, G. A., 58

BOROW, H., 87

BORUCH, R., 116, 117, 119, 127, 135

BRIMMER, A. F., 117

C

CALDWELL, E., 139

Career: choices of, 87, 88, 89; college degree and, 110; desirability of, 97–99; factors influencing selection of, 89, 90; restrictions on, 96–97; training for, 87. *See also* Salary, Jobs

Career aspirations, 91–92

Career preferences, 92–96

CARTER, T. P., 19

Center for Research and Development in Higher Education,

197